You Are Meant to Sing!

10 Steps to Unlock Your Inner Voice

Helane Marie Anderson

Copyright

Cover Design: AN Better Publishing

Editor: Elena Zaretsky

Author's photo courtesy of Katy Daixon Wimer

Advance Praise

This book, *You Are Meant to Sing!*, is not only an endearing story of Helane Marie Anderson's life and her successful search for her voice, it is also an essential guideline for finding *your* voice. Helane says "everyone is a singer." I believe it to be true! This self-help book gives you a treasure chest of tools and exercises that are outlined in a simple sequence. As we deconstruct the old and unwanted habits, memories, influences, etc., we also cultivate the new visions and dreams, highlighting the positive pieces of life that have always been part of the story. The new voice, the discovered voice, resounds fun, relief, and liberation. The ripples of each voice opening up to singing are phenomenal and far reaching. And what a timely recommendation by Helane when our country and our world need every bit of these ripples. This way, we indeed become the change we want for the world.

---Iva Nasr

Mentor, Speaker, Author of

From Rifles to Roses ~Memories and Miracles

In *You Are Meant To Sing!*, Helane Anderson describes the path to finding, listening to, and valuing your own voice. Using her own journey as a framework, Helane teaches the vital importance of personal voice and how to fully embrace this in your life. Chock full of heartfelt stories, useful strategies and loving guidance, she encourages ownership and expression of your voice in the manner best suited to your unique self. As Helane writes, we are ALL singers (joyous words to this only-in-the-car-alone singer). This book is a must-read for anyone who has ever felt unheard, misunderstood, or "not enough" – providing the information and encouragement necessary to stand up and step forward with confidence, letting *your* voice be heard.

--- Kristina Hallett, PhD, ABPP

Board Certified Clinical Psychologist, Speaker, Author of

Own Best Friend: Eight Steps to a Life of Purpose, Passion, and Ease

As a person who uses toning in spiritual practice, I am thrilled that this book, *You Are Meant to Sing! 10 Steps to Unlock Your Inner Voice* by Helane Marie Anderson, accompanies and enriches my journey! Through her own transformational experiences, Helane reveals the hidden truth behind our unheard voice and the inspirations we discover from listening to it. Step by step, she guides you to get in touch with your heart, connect with your soul, and blossom in your life all through your own voice. Our voice is a powerful tool to release whatever no longer serves us, help us heal from unwanted patterns, and create the infinite possibilities in our life with intention. This book is an invaluable resource to light up the path before you so that you can begin your journey, break away from all the conditions and stand up for who you truly are! i

---Jiayuh Chyan

Akashic Records Teacher, Multidimensional Healing Facilitator,

and Author of *Your Key to the Akashic Records*

Dedication

The book is dedicated to my mother with gratitude.

If our journey had been an easy one, this book would never exist, and the heart to serve never developed.

Thank you for the lessons and for being my greatest teacher in this life.

I love you.

Helane

Addendum:

At the time I finished the first draft manuscript of this book, I read my mother this dedication in person and it made her cry. Three months later, at the time I was focused on editing this book, my mother passed away. I will always be grateful for that time I had with her and that she knew about this dedication. It makes the journey of our relationship all that much more poignant.

Table of Contents

Preface

For the past six years I have taught a graduate course in Arts Leadership and Arts Entrepreneurship with Helane Anderson at the University of Southern California. The primary focus of the course has not been to train young artists and musicians to work in large organizations. The goal has been to help them create the institution necessary to realize their own artistic or cultural vision. I originally designed the course myself. I invited Helane to help with the intensive personal attention required to work with so many students at crucial stages of their careers.

Each year, however, as I watched Helane in action, I recognized her considerable gift helping students not simply develop but discover their life plans. In the arts, the goal of each person is different, especially when trying to create an organization to embody their individual needs and ambitions. It is impossible for students to plan until they realize exactly what it is they actually want. Not what their teachers or peers or parents want, but what inside them truly motivates their psyche. This mysterious self-exploration is the missing step in most graduate arts programs, which are better at technical instruction than elucidating the spiritual dimensions of the creative vocation.

Helane was so good at unlocking those ambitions and desires that each year I incorporated more of her methods in the course. Not surprisingly, the course became more effective in human terms. She had, I now realize, also helped me realize my own educational objectives of helping these talented graduate students envision and create their future. Her charismatic approach deepened the course's experiential power without losing its intellectual depth. I hope she has learned as much from me as I have from her.

Helane Anderson is a remarkable woman—a singer, pianist, mentor, and healer—who has developed her intuitive powers as capably as she trained her musical talents. The same qualities I saw so vividly in her classroom work are captured in this new book, *You Are Meant to Sing*! She understands the powers of self-discovery on the journey toward self-expression and self-realization. This book might be the first step for you on that journey.

Dana Gioia

Poet Laureate of California

Los Angeles, CA

Foreword

To The Reader About to Find Your Voice,

Helane is the perfect woman to help your transformation.

Growing up, as my cousin and Godmother (or Spirit Mother, as I like to call her), Helane always had the most poignant advice to trigger my spirit so I could find my own personal truth. Her suggestions for self-care practice helped stop the outside voices from ringing louder than my own. I always rose higher toward self-actualization after our long talks.

Despite living thousands of miles apart our entire lives, I always felt her love and support and carried it with me, especially in times of self-doubt. As a photographer and writer in rural Wisconsin documenting people's personal journeys, transformations and life shifts, I have experienced my own fair share of battling my internal dialogue with vocal and artistic expression. She was always there to help me figure out the best way to communicate my aspirations and reflect back to me what was working and what wasn't.

Over the New Year from 2015-2016, I took a brief reprieve from my life in Wisconsin and spent two weeks with Helane traveling in California.

I was burnt out. The life I was leading was based on fulfilling roles in my friendships and primary relationship that I thought were required of me. I was incredibly lost in my career, wanting desperately to speak loudly for myself and others through my creative projects, and feeling my current work endeavors were leaving me empty rather than fulfilled.

During our time together, Helane implemented (likely unknowingly) many of the tools you'll read in this book. The most memorable moment was making up a small song-like chant that felt almost Native American while relaxing on a rock in Joshua Tree National Park. She innately understood that even the tiniest of heart-filled expressions through the voice can open doors for personal understanding.

Helane led me to a place of greater understanding of who I am and what I'm meant to say and do in this world. And for that I am immensely grateful.

If you, in turn, open your heart to hearing Helane's journey and guidance throughout this fluid read, I promise you'll create the shifts you're seeking.

It worked for me.

Katy Daixon Wimer

Whitewater, WI

Introduction

"The human voice is the most perfect instrument of all."
– Arvo Pärt

The voice – *your* voice – is your primary instrument. It is your vehicle of communication and your main means of expression.

It is what gives songs to your soul.

To your inner spirit.

To your being.

It is what allows your emotions to be expressed, with and without words.

Think back to the moment you were born.

You likely came out crying, loudly expressing your disdain at leaving the womb and entering this world separate from your mother.

And you spend your life trying to reconnect.

Your voice is one of the primary tools you have been given for that purpose.

Yet how often have you heard the words "don't cry"?

So you shut yourself down and bottle your feelings.

What if, instead, you heard …

"Let it out."

"You have permission to feel exactly how you feel."

"Crying is a healthy release."

Perhaps you would be happy more consistently, able to move through emotions with more ease and express yourself without fear.

EVERYONE IS A SINGER

In workshops I teach I often ask the room, "Who here is a singer?"

Depending on the crowd, the raised hands can range from a couple of people to half of the room. And usually there are a few delayed hand raisers not ready to claim that "singer" is a part of their identity.

However, my strong belief and response is always that *EVERYONE* is a singer.

I can bet money on it that every person in that room has sung to "Don't Stop Believin'" on the radio, or curated a sing-a-long playlist for the shower or a road trip.

When I ask, "How many of you have ever sang along to your favorite tune on the radio, in the car, when you were alone?"

Every other person's hand in the room raises up.

And yes, this qualifies as being a singer.

Being a singer means singing.

Period.

Expressing oneself through song is using the voice to move energy and to develop connection with your inner self and others, even when doing it in your car for your own joyful purposes. You may have hidden singing from others, however now it is time to bring your voice out to the forefront and allow yourself the space to express yourself and be heard.

THE VOICE IS THE KEY TO CONNECTION THROUGH WORDS AND SOUND

Your voice, brain and the ability to communicate in a complicated fashion is what separates you from other life forms. In indigenous cultures around the globe, everyone sings regardless of the quality of each individual voice. Singing goes hand-in-hand with drumming, dancing and community engagement.

You are meant to sing and express yourself from a place of joy and connection: the voice is a tool in facilitating this. As a form of deep artistic and human expression, the singing voice is also meant to convey sadness, grief and despair. Any and all feelings can be expressed through singing and the voice. In fact, singing and communicating the range of human emotions will help your energy move and allow you to connect more deeply with others. Sharing yourself in musical communion and song with others, even through the difficult times, is powerful medicine.

Alternatively, shutting down your self-expression and suppressing your natural singing voice can result in multiple physical complications such as: throat infections, including strep throat, tonsillitis, laryngitis; problems in the cervical vertebrae leading to neck tension; headaches; neck and jaw pain; TMJ; and allergies. It can cause you to continually get choked up when trying to express feelings, to feel shut down emotionally, mentally and physically, and it can show up as isolation, stress and sadness.

Singing can help you move through both physical and mental challenges once you find an outlet that works for you. The exercises I have laid out in this book will help facilitate this. They are designed to bring you back to your internal bond with your voice, give you ideas for finding the shared experience of singing with and in front of people and bring you back to a place of connection.

And feeling that connection with your inner self and shared human experience is where the primal wound of separation from the mother is healed.

SINGING AND CONNECTION TO THE HIGHER SELF OR THE DIVINE

Every religion in our culture includes some type of singing or vocal recitation as an expression of mysticism and connection to the divine or the "higher self".

In Jewish traditions, singing is an integral part of sacred services.

Christianity utilizes many musical forms, including hymns, chants and psalms.

Muslim worship is centered around reciting prayers five times a day.

Chanting is an integral part of Buddhism and Hinduism.

Indigenous cultures use the voice, music and dancing with drums and instruments like the didgeridoo for healing and rituals.

So, given that singing is an ingrained part of the collective of human history and communing, how can you bring that practice into your daily life to reap the benefits of using your voice? Let's dig a bit further.

Singing is a part of Western culture, though the first documented singing (according to music history texts) was based in a church setting beginning with Gregorian chant and sacred music. Though beautiful, the nature of this music is precise, with room for improvisation, and was notated to be preserved and shared with other churches for worship purposes. Secular music existed through Troubadour songs set to poems that were also notated with room for improvisation.

Notating music for the sake of history and sharing has its place in all musical traditions, though in these earlier eras from the Medieval through the Romantic period improvisation was always also a part of performance practice. Bach, Beethoven, Mozart and Liszt all combined improvisation with notated music. Singers also improvised during those eras, as it was part of their training. However, as Western music evolved, improvisation became much less a part of the training and intention.

Classical performers rarely improvise in their training today, so an element of that connection to the "pure" or "raw" voice is often lost in the classical music world now. Jazz, rock and other types of music do utilize this practice more regularly and the freedom within the performance is felt.

In my own practice, I find that improvising with my voice has helped my classical singing voice become more versatile and free, and difficult technical things have actually become easier rather than more difficult. I encourage you to also experiment and challenge your voice by developing this daily practice.

As you prepare to explore your voice more fully, take a moment to identify the way you currently like to express your voice:

What genres of music do you feel particularly drawn to?

Which types of music do you most enjoy singing?

Have you improvised music with your voice before?

Whatever type of music you prefer, I propose that you start working with your voice by connecting with your raw instrument in the way of bringing forth any energy inside of you without judgment. This means making stuff up with your voice and letting the emotions within you be expressed in whatever way they come out. You don't have to subscribe to any particular type of religious belief or musical style to do this exercise – it is about connecting to what's inside of you first and foremost.

Once you have done this, go back and revisit the music you enjoy singing most and notice if it feels different or if your voice feels stronger.

The time feels ripe to bring more of your vocal energy and expression back into your self-expression. In this way you can draw upon your daily life and make improvising with your voice and singing part of voicing your truth.

CULTIVATING THE COURAGE TO EXPRESS YOUR VOICE

Speaking up and singing out takes courage. And it's hard.

I know for me, both in school and in life, I was often told to tone my voice down or be more passive. So over the years I silenced parts of my voice that are only now coming up to the surface. "Don't rock the boat!" echoed in my ears.

Putting yourself on the stage for the world to see is especially courageous and, no matter what you do, there will always be some backlash. Understanding your innermost truth and singing from this place will free you from fear of being judged.

People's judgments are always about their own reality anyways, both positive and negative. If you can listen to your own needs and trust that what you are expressing comes from an innate place of wisdom within, you won't be deterred by others judgments, or your own.

But you cannot free yourself until you learn to work with your own critical inner voices, the voices you have let be louder than all the others for such a long time. And then, from this new state, you learn to have integrity with your own internal dialogue.

I am often drawn back to Don Miguel Ruiz's *The Four Agreements* and his statement to "be impeccable with your word." I believe it is possible to be impeccable with your thoughts as well as your words and, as humans, there is much work to be done.

Often parents speak about how much easier parenting gets once a child can speak and tell them what it wants, if it's hungry, upset or tired. And parents give direction in that process. So you grow up being told when to speak, how to speak, what's appropriate when, how to choose your words and, in many cases, instructed to never tell people how you are really feeling.

Think about your response when someone at work greets you in the morning with, "Hi, how are you?"

Can you imagine saying, "I feel a little ashamed right now and upset at myself that I was late this morning"?

When people ask how you are, you are generally expected to give a generic "I'm fine", even if the response is not truth. But if you are not genuinely being honest then your voice gets lost.

Once my mother told me that at dinner parties, politics and religion were off limits for conversation. Given that my mom leaned politically left and my dad towards the right, I can understand why. However, I welcome those discussions, even when people are on different sides of the fence. It's about being mindful, respectful and clear.

You and I are not meant to agree on everything.

In order to facilitate understanding and truth, you must open the space up for discussion without judgment. Your beliefs are a make-up of your life experience and what you have been taught through societal conditioning. Sharing those beliefs is part of connecting with your voice.

Vocal expression is a way of taking yourself back to your truth.

So what does this have to do with singing, you might ask?

Everything.

THE PROCESS OF HEALING THE VOICE

It is my passion and purpose to help more people speak their truth, to transform and become the best versions of who they are. I personally feel this is accomplished through the voice and learning how to communicate in a way that enhances all areas of your life, both personal and professional.

In my years working with clients in sound and energy healing, I have pieced together tools from my studies, as well as my own experiments, and provide them as exercises here to align the voice with the body. You can use them when needed, in order or at your own pace.

Through toning, singing, sounding, breathing, chanting and speaking, your voice can transform your life into the full authentic expression of who you are meant to become. The exercises will take you through emotional places, unblock your stuck places and support your growth and sense of well-being.

I begin by addressing the blocks that lie beneath the surface of your expression, and develop your confidence to unleash your gift to the world. You will learn tools and ways to practice singing in a way to heal yourself and others and connect with your spirit.

The transformation process will not always be easy. It will put you up against your triggers and will bring to the surface anything getting in the way of your joyful vocal expression. It will take work and I will be there to support your process.

You are ready to sing again!

And, together, we will get to the other side.

And soon you will hear...

That small voice, barely an audible whisper.

The shy one in the corner without the courage to come out.

It will begin to speak.

It will get louder.

"I know why I'm here."

"I know what I'm doing."

"I'm redefining my happiness."

And then the song comes in to drown the critical inner voices out.

Pharrell Williams' *Happy* comes on the radio.

And then ...

That voice decides to sing along.

The person next to you chimes in, too, and the dance starts.

People look at you funny, but you don't care because you are happy and the joy in you exudes to others.

You remember a fundamental need that is unfulfilled and needs to be brought back to the surface. Shared. Utilized.

Your voice, your joy, your community, your connection.

If only you could get out of your own way and own it. Be it.

Loud, proud and vibrant.

Fully in your joy and self-expression.

Connected to others and the divine through the power of the voice.

Your voice.

It's time to allow the expression of your inner beauty and being to shine forth and be shared!

Let's not waste any more time and get started!

Your joyful expression awaits you.

> *"The lotus flower blooms from the deepest and thickest mud."*
> --Buddhist Proverb

Chapter 1 – The Journey

The story of a voice

"Maybe the journey isn't about becoming anything.
Maybe it's about un-becoming everything that isn't really you so you
can be who you were meant to be in the first place."

\- Anonymous

THE HEART OF A PERFORMER

"Can I sing and dance for you?" was often heard coming out of my mouth as a toddler.

Strangers in the grocery store, my parents' friends, extended family... basically, anyone who would sit through my elaborate productions where I dressed up my brothers and sang and danced were all subjected to my voice. And it was very important to me that everyone turn their focus to me and listen.

I had the heart of a performer and wanted to share.

But at the age of nine, my mother explained to me that I had a "child's voice" and that I would never be a real singer. She wanted to save me from disappointment and she didn't understand that some voices took time to fully develop.

My brain believed what she said but my soul still didn't listen.

To me, vocal expression was a natural part of my being. Like most of you, I emerged from the womb crying with gusto. My lungs were strong and so was my voice. I had a lot to say and crying was the only expression available as a new human.

According to my family, I pretty much cried the first two years of my life. As an empathic child, that is not surprising as I absorbed everyone else's pain and suffering and my small shell needed to get that out somehow.

The crying was too much for my mother, a woman who was 24 and suffering from severe Endometriosis, bipolar disorder and manic depression in a world that taught her to keep things silent. She felt no safety in self-expression and subconsciously passed that fear along to me.

And at that time, to avoid flipping an emotional switch, she did the best thing she could think of and locked me in a room until I stopped crying. I learned that not only was it not OK to cry, but that it was not safe to feel and express how I felt.

But that still didn't stop me. I still wanted to sing.

I got used to being misunderstood and learned from my mother and schoolmates that standing out or expressing who I really was wasn't safe. My belief was that fully sharing would only bring me pain. And after that comment at age nine, I only half shared, and the full joy of vocal expression died.

But instead of completely shutting down, I sang through the pain of never believing I was good or good enough. And these self-doubts manifested in overcompensation.

I became the teacher's pet in my new school in North Carolina and was featured in an article about problems with the school system – in other words, a complete set-up for being highly disliked by my peers.

I played the piano for the chorus and sang, being consistently recognized for my gifts by my teachers. And the more it happened, the more I became susceptible to ridicule and an easy target for mean girls.

I never spoke up for myself and took the abuse, not realizing that – on some level – I was learning to shut my voice down even further. Often the bullying in school mirrored the books I read, in Judy

Blume's *Blubber* fashion.

I literally had "kick me" signs put on my back.

A part of me accepted that this was going to be my fate at the ripe age of twelve. I was meant to be unpopular and alone.

I remained silent (except for the crying) and turned to music as my escape and my solace. The music drowned out the voices that echoed my mother, the voices that echoed the bullying, the voices that I began to internalize. Music silenced the voices that whispered to me ...

"Just keep silent and take it."

"You deserve the punishment."

"You are not good enough."

The louder voices scolded ...

"Who are you to perform?"

"No one will love you if you let yourself be fully seen."

"It's not OK to be vulnerable."

"If you are vulnerable, you will only experience more pain."

"STAY QUIET OR ELSE!"

So many voices yelled at me internally that I couldn't decipher which ones belonged to my "true self".

HOW THE LOUD VOICES MANIFESTED

All of my internal conflicts manifested physically, as they often do. I had migraine headaches that started at age ten, irritable bowel syndrome, bleeding ulcers causing me to be on the verge of a blood transfusion at seventeen and numerous gynecological issues resulting in five surgeries, including one for inherited Endometriosis.

Anxiety about making a mistake plagued me, anxiety that I wouldn't be good enough, that I would never catch up, that someone might actually find me out!

I honestly don't think I really experienced a moment of true internal peace in my childhood – the voices were just too damn loud!

Eventually, music – which had been my saving grace up to that point – began to lose its soothing effect. I still sang, and even went on to take voice lessons in high school, college, throughout graduate school and beyond. But the music ceased to be fully connected to my soul.

How can it be connected when the intention and underlying emotion is stemmed in pain?

So I escaped to a boxed-in version of music where perfectionism ran rampant. I shut down the improvisatory creative music side that once came so naturally to me and embarked on the classical music path. Slowly, the joy started leaving the experience altogether.

I loved it, or so I said, but music and singing became much more a mental brain exercise and inner gymnastics than a true expression of what was in my heart.

I never felt good enough, like my voice wasn't developed enough, that everyone was better than me and that I didn't have enough to offer. And, as the years progressed, I became immersed in the classical music world, finding the dynamic of playing the piano easier than putting my voice first and foremost.

The classical music world is highly critical and perfectionism is a given. Even though I consistently performed, every single time I was up on stage I had voices telling me I wasn't good enough, that I was going to make a mistake and that everyone would think my performance was bad.

But really that was all just an echo of what I thought about myself. And this anxiety manifested as an overwhelming presence every time I performed, so that rather than music creation echoing the expression of what was deep in my soul, it became an exercise in "getting through" the performance. Rather than sharing the music from a heart-centered place, I was simply in my head trying to quiet the voices.

Even though I continued to perform in some capacity, I decided to go the "music business" route to save myself from further criticism. I spent years building up a career created by convention and perceived stability, supporting other people's careers in the music industry and stifling my own creativity in the process. It was my "shadow career," a career built out of my own fears and those pressed upon me.

However, I did love being a part of the Classical Music world and most of my friends were musicians, so my choice to develop as an Arts Administrator felt like a good option. I was good at the business side of things and it felt easier for me at the time. I chose safety rather than pursuing what was in my heart.

I pushed my own innate creative inclinations down and decided to get my M.A. in Arts Administration so that I could continue to be a part of the industry. It was easier for me to be in the position of judging and hiring everyone else rather than putting my own creativity on the line. The critical ear and inner voices became an innate part of my job, and I could use them while judging others instead of myself.

Those critical voices were put to good use in that role.

However, my deeper internal voice – the one wanting to express the music inside of me – shut down because I did not feel free to create, lest I put myself on the chopping block as a subject for criticism: the same criticism that I was dishing out to others.

I made these choices out of fear.

Ultimately, I became so emotionally blocked that when I actually did sing or perform, it was a reflection of blockages – a voice without a soul – an instrument trying to do everything perfectly with technique but no real expression of love, tenderness or feeling underneath it. I was highly functioning and productive, doing what needed to be done. But I was desperate to be heard. And I had lost my joy.

BREAKDOWN TO BREAKTHROUGH

The turning point came when I grew into highly desired positions as a music administrator and was on track towards achieving my (inauthentic) goal to run a major arts institution in the United States. My father was diagnosed with Pancreatic Cancer and died, just as I was moving to my "dream job" in Los Angeles working at the Los Angeles Philharmonic programming concerts at the Hollywood Bowl and Walt Disney Concert Hall.

And slowly, through my grief and a very demanding job, I found myself faced with the demons and voices I hadn't listened to in years. Some would call it a spiritual crisis.

I call it an awakening

Internally I had hit rock bottom. And I mean: Rock. Bottom.

I was struck with the flu, a cough that wouldn't go away, the return of old serious health issues and depression. I was seeing a counselor who sent me to a psychiatrist who was ready to write me sick leave from work and wrote me a prescription for Zoloft.

Alongside losing my father, I truly believe it was the suppression of my voice that caused the depression – not feeling heard, understood or able to speak my truth without fear.

After about a month on the anti-depressants I started to feel numb and noticed how my body and mind were actually just suppressing the emotions and truths I needed to face and deal with. I began researching ways to cure depression by natural methods and decided to go away for a week to do a juice fast at Big Bear Mountain. I read that juice fasting was the quickest way to clear depression and, though I wasn't sure if I could live a week without actual food, I was ready to try anything.

Even though I went on restrictive food diets in the past, this was the first time I truly experienced the "detox" portion of cleansing. And I don't mean just the physical symptoms: the detox symptoms also included intense emotional release. I knew this would happen to some extent, but I was not prepared for what came up.

With all of the stuff I had been through, I thought I would cry a lot and go deeper into sadness. However, anger was the prevalent force that surfaced: an anger I had never experienced before. This was an anger deep in my bones that began to bubble like lava ready to erupt and destroy everything in its wake. And I didn't cry the whole week.

Physically I felt very hungry by the fifth day and almost didn't make it through the full cleanse. But I did make it and, by the end, I felt lighter and clearer than I ever had before, and I mean EVER.

I turned the corner at this point. I now knew there were things I could do to heal myself and face the things I needed to face. And the self-care I embraced to heal my own depression naturally helped me access my personal power again. I was ready to embark on the path of healing.

The depression was cleared. But I still had lots of work to do.

Another year passed in that space and I felt better, yet that tugging was still at my soul. Though there were elements of my job I found rewarding, I still wasn't happy.

There was a tornado of fear around voicing this truth. I knew that if anyone found out, I was completely vulnerable to losing my job to someone more ambitious than myself. Someone more like the old me rather than the new me – the sad, lost, confused, depressed me.

Fast-forward to the summer of 2009 and everything began breaking down. I went on a retreat in the spring that completely changed me. I did such deep internal process work that, for the first time, I saw clearly all of the things that were not working in my life. My motivations were shifting and changing. I had completely suppressed my singing voice and I was deeply unhappy.

I was not an easy person to be around during this period. Many friends from that time faded away and, though some of that was painful, I know now it was simply divine order and necessary to propel me to find the people who understood and saw me. The real me.

Alongside a deep desire to reconnect with my voice, I finally understood that for years I'd been hiding my deep intuition, my empathy, my psychic visions and the fact that I could perceive and take on people's pain with a simple touch or hug. I was hiding because I didn't understand the inherent nature of my gifts or capabilities. I really didn't know what I was experiencing or how to separate my own emotions from others'. Everyone's stuff stuck to me like glue and I was depressed, overwhelmed and at a loss as to what to do about it.

So I reached out for help.

I spent the next decade doing anything and everything I could do to heal myself so I could help others do the same. I journeyed to the jungles of Peru and looked deeply into my own bouts of depression, what caused them, how much I was shut down to my joy and happiness. I came face to face with what my soul wanted and saw that I was meant to be in the healing profession, rather than at the service of artists in the classical music industry.

I was ready to change but deeply afraid.

The internal voices screamed again:

"Who are you to do this?

You're going to be poor!

You're never going to succeed!"

These big voices were LOUD and my brain rationalized how I was going to stay where I was in St. Paul (where I had only been at a new job for six months) until the end of the year, leaving everything in a clean place.

As divine timing would have it, on the second day back to work from a soul-searching trip, I was fired. Deemed not a fit – *from both ends* – though at the time I was reluctant to admit it.

We hid the fact I was let go and spun my moving back to California under a guise of "pursuing other interests", which is known corporate-speak for "fired". My ego felt like raw beaten eggs being cooked on hot pavement.

Who was I if not the talented artistic administrator in my chosen field slated to run a major arts institution?

Who would ever hire me again?

Who was I if everyone actually KNEW that I had FAILED?

My ego took a major beating. I prided myself on how good I was at my job, at connecting people and organizing major projects. My entire identity was tied up with the way I perceived myself in relation to my work. And I relied on others' opinions of me to define how I felt about myself. So facing this meant all the beliefs I had internalized and created were untrue. So who was I then?

I couldn't take it and I hid the truth. I needed my dignity intact. But as divine intelligence would have it, my internal strife began reflecting in my external world and the 180-degree (much-needed) shift began to unfold.

With the new understanding that I was an empath and needed to embrace my healing intuitive abilities, I took the most logical next step. Armed with a recent yoga teacher training certification (completed with the original intent of simply deepening my practice), the healing path unfolded as I signed up to become a certified massage and CranioSacral therapist.

Every session through healing and training (both given and received) taught me something new, healed something different, and I saw how we as humans are always like onions, continually peeling off layers, getting to a deeper core of what lies underneath the surface. Every step was another layer, another understanding, another tool, another gift, another letting go, all leading me closer and closer to working with sound and my voice. I knew that my path involved music and healing. But I didn't know what that meant or how it was to unfold.

I continued singing as a soprano soloist at a church in Santa Monica, keeping my voice connected to my classical self, and slowly built my healing practice through part-time massage jobs and further studies in healing work. I continued adding tools to my toolbox.

The internal shifts felt subtle at first and then began moving faster. A pinnacle point happened through a revelation I had during an advanced Polarity Therapy class. I was given an exercise about values and challenged with identifying my purpose and mission in this life. Though healing is most definitely one of my callings and why I was in the class to begin with, it became clear that MUSIC was and is my first love. It's what connects me to my internal joy. Through this exercise, I realized the core of who I am: A Musician.

With this realization, I changed my priorities again and finally went to sound healing training in San Francisco at the Globe Institute. From that point forward, my life was changed. Through the workshops and teachings I experienced in those intense four weeks of nine hours of class each day, I saw everything I was meant to be doing with clarity.

All the healing work finally came together in a space that

utilized all of my passions in one place: music, public speaking, connecting people, energy healing, teaching, singing, movement and dancing.

And my voice cracked open.

CRACKED open!

For the first time in my life, I was able to transcend all the fears, perfectionism and control to unleash my true instrument. And my truth came soaring out of me. My clarity came through my singing voice.

It was not conventional, it was not perfect, it was imperfectly perfect – it was the voice of my soul. FINALLY coming out to play.

And this is the gift I am ready now to share with you. To help you find your own gift and make it heard with pride and confidence: a pure reflection of you.

As a wise friend once said to me, "Great leaders don't create followers, they create other great leaders."

May my personal journey inspire you to uncover your true voice, so you can become the light you are meant to be.

It's time.

THE SINGING TOOLBOX

WRITE YOUR STORY

Step 1. Take some time to write down why you want to sing and use your voice. I suggest 1-2 pages. Free write without judging if you can.

Step 2. Write about what you feel made your voice shut down in the past.

Describe the feeling, circumstances and people.

Be vulnerable with yourself and be raw.

Step 3. Really take your time with this. Identifying where you are now is important before you move forward. This will give you a measure of progress with your voice and your story as you embark upon this journey of unlocking what lies within.

Chapter 2 – Are you a Victim, Survivor or Transformer?

Personal Mantras and the Power of our Words

*"It's not about perfect. It's about effort.
And when you bring that effort every single day, that's where
transformation happens. That's how change occurs."*

— Jillian Michaels

Are you a victim, survivor or transformer?

It is a question that I ask my clients often as a way of identifying the state they are currently in.

A victim blames others for their problems and takes no responsibility.

A survivor moves through the motions of life without really fully living or utilizing what they've learned, operating from a place of wounding.

A transformer takes the experiences of the past and molds it into lessons that enhance, inspire, create and help others.

Let me tell you how this manifested in my own journey, how I came to understand these different roles, and how I embodied each one of them.

THE VICTIM

Most of my life I was a survivor, though often I took on the role of victim.

In the victim state, I blamed my mother for everything. It was her fault that my life was so difficult because she abused me emotionally. She openly criticized me whenever she had the chance. It was her fault that I felt so alone, that I didn't have anyone on my side, that I had so many relationship issues.

I often watched how nice she was to people outside of the family, and then wondered why she was so mean to me. She showed affection only by giving gifts and often praised me in front of others to make her look good, but privately showed little affection.

It was the only way she knew how to express herself.

And I told this story to anyone who got close enough to me to listen. In essence, I was perpetuating my victim state by telling the story of emotional abuse in a way that made me less responsible for any problems I had in my life.

It was *her* fault things in my life were messed up, not mine.

At the time, I did not understand how every single time I told this story, I was perpetuating the pain of a life experience I desperately wanted to let go of. Sure, my mother wasn't perfect, but as a fully-grown woman, I was responsible for why this pattern was continually repeating itself.

In order to change my life, I had to reframe my story and tell it with the energy of a lesson learned, rather than a reaction to the pain. I had to access and change my voice with words and it took time and discipline. I tried many things to shift this energy, however it was the practice of working with mantras that helped me get there the fastest. I will get more into what mantras are and how they work shortly, however the importance of sharing this now is that the meaning of the words of the mantra I chose embodies taking responsibility for one's own actions and for forgiveness of yourself and others.

The power of the words of this particular mantra – I'm Sorry. Please Forgive Me. Thank you. I Love You. – actually worked. I didn't feel the effects right away, but with regular practice I noticed that I was able to shift how I related to my mother through finally practicing forgiveness and taking responsibility for my own actions and reactions.

THE SURVIVOR

To give you a glimpse of where I came from and how shut down I was, let me take you back to a traumatic time that defined much of my adult life. This event was the primary reason I struggled with relationships and with trust.

When I was 25, I clicked into survivor mode after my mother tried to take her life. I did not have the tools to process what happened or understand the severity of her depression, so I turned to the one thing I knew how to do as exampled by my father: Work.

Neither my Dad, brothers nor I had the tools at the time to handle the reality of what just happened, so we all manifested different ways of coping that did not include talking about it or relying on each other.

Survival mode manifested as obsessive fastidiousness and workaholism for me. It became my default reaction when someone or something disappointed me and I poured myself wholeheartedly into work. It was a safe place where I did not have to face my emotional wounding.

However, perfectionism ran rampant in that space. I beat myself up for any and every mistake that I made, and the people on the outside, meaning those I worked for, reflected that.

I defined myself by my success and told the story of my career often because that story was easier to tell than going into the story of what was beneath that choice. My ambition drove my choices and masked the pain. It certainly was easier than dealing with what happened with my mother and the broken state of my family in the aftermath.

Everything else took a backseat to my career and the driving force was simply survival, so I shut down the internal shifting voice drawn to the healing arts and my own music.

I embodied both the survivor and the victim at the same time, until I finally learned how to transform that energy and belief system.

THE TRANSFORMER

It took many years of spiritual practice for me to even realize that I was in survivor mode, but once I did, I became obsessed with how I could change this state of being and shift it into another place. This began with addressing how I used my voice to create my present and future life experience. I eventually shifted how I told the story of what happened with my mom and what happened with my career. I learned how to forgive, let go and transform.

And I did this with my voice, mantra practice, writing and word choices.

Now the story I tell is how much I learned from my mother and how she was the most important spiritual teacher for me in this lifetime. If I had an easy relationship with her, I never would have embarked upon my spiritual quest and journey, which has brought me here to this point. It is our complicated mother-daughter relationship that caused me to lose my voice and to journey far and wide to find it again.

In terms of the story I tell about my career, the truth is that I had a much greater calling with my healing work than to continue living behind the scenes in the classical music world. The difficulties in my past work life are what pushed me to find my true path.

And that is how I became a transformer.

And you can too.

My deepest intention is to demonstrate how you can use your words to change your story, change your perspective and change your life. The power is within you even if you don't always feel you have access to it. Those are the moments to reach out and ask for some help and guidance to get there, or you can use the tools throughout this book to express your own voice through practice.

You will also need patience. Transformation takes patience and persistence. Showing up with a willingness to do the work and get down to business.

Change does not happen while twiddling your thumbs. It happens when you continue to show up and move through life's challenges.

Some questions to ask yourself as you prepare to dive in:

What traumas caused you to shut your voice down?

What is a common element in your difficult relationships?

Can you tell a transformative story about anything in your past?

This book is meant to help you identify the core answers to these questions and give you tools to help you turn your life around. It also offers methods for using your voice to bring lasting change for yourself and others.

Like the butterfly that emerges from the darkness of the cocoon, you just have to trust and be with the darkness until it lifts.

And those voices, the ones that kept you from singing aloud all along. Those are the ones that are going to become louder now. Those voices will try to stop you in your tracks and make you question your choice to start singing again. And you will learn to listen to them, work with them, use them and ultimately transform them into a place that will increase your vocal abilities.

Let me share how the loud voices tried to stop me from my dream and how I pushed through them.

THE PROCESS OF SHARING MY VOICE

The first sound healing album I recorded went very well in the studio. Improvised, yet structured, the five tracks worked their way through the elements: ether, air, water, earth and fire, and I recorded them with my friends on violin and drums. It was the moment I transformed my classical singing and music background into the creation of music with the intent to heal.

I was proud of what we did.

However, once I got into the listening process of editing, those familiar critical perfectionist voices reemerged and wanted to fix everything, make everything different, change a note, alter the structure. My classical music brain heard every perceived imperfection – all things that defied the whole purpose of recording an improvised track.

Anxiety dreams and the loud voices screamed at night, worries of what people would think and how I would be judged. Alas, the voices became louder as I followed my vision to fruition. They wanted to stop me from presenting my gifts to the world and allowing my true voice to be heard, utilized and shared with others.

The stories from the critics inside my head grew louder and more forceful with every step as I got closer to my dreams of releasing this album to the world. Thankfully, my courage also grew and the desire to share my voice became stronger.

One method I used to strengthen my resolve was that I began a dialogue with the critical voices and brought them into focus to listen to them. At the moment I was finally able to let them voice their concerns to me in an objective way, they eventually began to subside. The voices telling me the CD wasn't good enough were fearful and I wanted no part of that. I wanted to share this music as a first offering of what was to come and I allowed the voices telling me to push through the insecurities to become louder.

And I'm so glad I did! Releasing the CD has gone on to serve my clients in a positive way and I'm proud of that.

This internal dialogue of simultaneously critical and encouraging voices still comes up when I am getting ready to do something new and sing in another arena. So what do I do when they resurface?

I make space to listen to them, hear them out. And then I make them listen to me after I calm them and let them know I am choosing to go in another direction. With practice, the voices get quieter and more still. My loud yelling voices have become so much softer and more trusting that I am now a different person, and no longer let my fears get in the way.

My favorite visual for illustrating this is from the cartoon *The Flintstones*. If you ever watched that cartoon, you will remember Fred Flintstone's internal dilemmas getting worked out between the devil on one shoulder and the angel on the other shoulder. They often argued and disagreed, but ultimately Fred had to choose which one to listen to.

And you will learn to do the same.

As you move through this singing process, the way you frame your own story will shift and change. You will do this by shifting your story into tales of transformation and incorporating mantra practice. And through these actions, the connection from your head to your heart to your vocal chords will emerge.

MANTRA PRACTICE

So what are mantras?

Mantras are words that can be said or sung that carry the vibration of what it is you desire and are calling into your life. In addition to changing how you tell your story, regular mantra practice will help you move from victim to survivor to transformer.

The first known mantras are in Sanskrit and are around 3,000 years old [1], some with actual words and some carrying more vibrational energy with syllables. There are many popular ancient mantras in Sanskrit, however mantras can be done and created in any language that resonates with you.

Mantras are extremely effective tools for shifting patterns and a very important practice to bring singing into your daily life. In fact, I believe that this is the most effective tool in working with the voice. Mantras and words carry vibration and, with continued discipline and practice, have the power to shift any pattern in the body, no matter how deeply imbedded it is.

For me, singing, speaking and creating mantras, along with changing the framework of my personal story, played a huge role in my transformation. This practice changed my life.

One of the most powerful things you can do to begin this internal change is to work with mantras directly. For the sake of this practice, I recommend mixing both existing Sanskrit and your own personal mantras in whatever is your native language. Knowing and choosing a mantra based on your personal intention is important for working with the voice in this capacity.

Our words carry vibration and energy.

By reaffirming a positive statement that expresses what we are underneath the limited belief or negative thought, we, in essence, begin to change our neuro-programs and the energy and vibration becomes an embodiment of the new thought.

Sound amplifies this change.

If you've read books in the realm of self-help or personal development, you know that they often focus on positive affirmations as powerful tools. Through singing these positive

---

[1] Frits Staal (1996), Rituals and Mantras, Rules without meaning, ISBN 978-8120814127, Motilal Banarsidass

words, the sound created within our body changes our structure and brain state in profound ways and amplifies the intention and experience.

In working with different Sanskrit mantras, I've noticed the subtle shifts in myself and subsequent major shifts as I alternate them. It is important to choose one mantra that speaks to you most at any given time and really focus on it for a 40-day period of time.

It is believed that it takes a minimum of 40 days for the energy of a mantra to take hold in your system and clear the energy that has been blocked from that manifestation. The commitment of the 40 days is important, and you can continue your chosen mantra after this time, or choose a new one if you sense your desired feeling state was achieved.

The second step in this process is to repeat the mantra 108 times for each of the 40 days, easily done with a set of mala beads.

Why 108 times?

The number 108 has many different meanings and significances. The Sun's diameter is 108 times the Earth's diameter, the Sun's distance from the Earth is 108 times the diameter of the Sun and the distance between the Moon and the Earth is 108 times the diameter of the Moon. In astrology, there are 12 houses and 9 planets and 12x9=108. In sacred geometry, the Sri Yantra symbol includes 54 intersecting lines, which are said to represent the male and the female, resulting in 108, and the angles of the lines of a pentagon are exactly 108 degrees. Finally, in sound healing, 108 is a multiple of 432, which is said to be the hertz measurement (pitches in sound are measured in hertz) of the most healing "A" in the tonal system. Western tuning generally measures the "A" at 440hz.

And what is a mala?

A mala is a beaded necklace that contains 108 beads and can also be worn as a bracelet. To make it easy, mala beads are readily available online or at any spiritual bookstore. I highly suggest buying mala beads since almost all mala beads have exactly 108 beads, so it makes it easy to count (some have more or half so just make sure the one you purchase has 108).

And now it is time to choose your mantra.

THE SINGING TOOLBOX

CHOOSING YOUR MANTRA

Step 1. Focus in on the one thing you would like to shift in your life, or what energy you would like more of in your life.

Step 2. Look for a mantra that carries this intention. You can choose your personal mantra created from the guided meditation available online through streaming on my website, or choose any of the suggested mantras that you feel drawn to from the list below. You can also go on YouTube to look up the Sanskrit pronunciation of any of the mantras listed below.

My First Personal Mantra:

"I am beautiful as I am, embodiment of the divine. Love and light and all that is intertwined."

While studying sound healing at the Globe Sound and Consciousness Institute, I developed this personal mantra as a song. At the time it was aspirational, as I wasn't fully feeling the words. However, as I started to sing the words, I began to embody the sentiment.

It's really important to own the state as an "I am" statement rather than "I hope to", "I need to", "I try to", " I want to" and even "I aspire to". In the development of your own mantra, you must word it to be in the present, as if you are already there. And thinking in the terms of Quantum Physics, you already are.

"Om Mani Padme Hum" – Roughly translated as "The Jewel in the heart of the Lotus"

This chant comes from the goddess Kuan Yin and invokes mercy and compassion, and unconditional love for yourself and others.

I used this mantra when I first embarked on my sound healing journey. Over the course of the 40 days I noticed a very subtle shift into peacefulness. This mantra helped me understand that my body had continuously been in fight or flight and needed the help to simply relax and be.

This mantra is very powerful for accessing a peaceful state of mind.

"Om"

Om is the sound of creation, the first sound of the universe. Just chanting Om by itself is a powerful grounding force that connects us to the divine. Comprised of three sounds, "ah – oo – ohm", it brings the energy back to the present, which is why it is so effective at the beginning and end of a yoga class, or any type of workshop with sound.

"Om Gam Ganapatayah Namaha"

The mantra calls upon the elephant god Ganesh, remover of obstacles. This is a great one for moving past blocked energy and getting out of your own way to create what you desire in your life.

"I'm sorry. Please forgive me. Thank you. I love you"

This mantra, known as Ho'ponopono, comes from the Hawaiian Shamanistic tradition and focuses on the forgiveness of yourself and others. Whenever I am having conflicts with people, I draw this mantra out as a great tool, like I did with my mother. When chanting, you are taking responsibility for any part in yourself that is creating the conflict and, in essence, shifting it around.

"Om Tare Tuttare Soha"

A devotional chant to the goddess Tara, this mantra is used for liberation from the seven limbs of fear.

Chanting this particular mantra actually brought my fears to the surface, before they cleared. Sometimes sound and vibration does this – brings to the surface those things that are ready to release. It's important to be aware of this in the healing process. Often with clients, the muscle knot or emotional blockage clears as soon as the connection to what caused it is identified.

This mantra is very powerful for dealing with and facing fears, but it is not for the faint of heart.

"Om Namah Shivaya"

This is a mantra to Lord Shiva, which focuses on relieving physical and mental ailments and restoring the being to a state of peace. This is powerful for healing any type of sickness. I used this mantra before and after I had surgery and it helped aid the healing process. It also helped me face the pain head-on in order to let my body heal.

"Aum Bhur Bhuvah Swah, Tat Savitur Varenyam, Bhargo Devasya Dhimahi, Dhiyo Yo Nah Prachodayat"

The Gayatri Mantra is about true liberation and connection to the divine.

When in Egypt in March 2016 for the Spring Equinox, we sang this mantra in the King's Chamber of the Great Pyramid and I started sobbing. This mantra is truly powerful and magical – for me it was about receiving, entering in the flow and letting go.

Step 3. Whatever mantra you choose, make sure you resonate with the intention of what you are bringing into your life and that you enjoy singing the words. You will know when the words resonate. Also, keep in mind that different mantras work at different times.

In my practice, I work with clients on choosing the best personal mantras for the present moment. May this practice help you shift your words and begin to access your voice to sing from your heart-centered space.

Chapter 3 – Preparing to Unleash Your Voice to the World

"A journey of a thousand miles must begin with a single step."
– Lao Tzu

LOOKING WITHIN

On the surface, singing comes across as an external process since it's the outward part of the sharing that people first experience. However, the quality of the voice, the emotions conveyed through the voice and the overall human connection felt by the listener stem from everything residing within you.

The first part of knowing yourself intimately is to silence the clutter of the externals and the mind, to develop awareness of what you are conveying to others and to listen to your internal voice: the one that speaks in the silences. Experiencing that silence and stillness and observing what lies within is the key. Then you will have awareness.

Usually when you begin to enter silence or a meditation practice, you may notice that the first thoughts that come up are chaotic and bombard your brain. This is often referred to as "monkey mind" – thoughts that are set on repeat like a record that skips.

It is in observing these thoughts and listening to them that they eventually become quiet. And once they get quiet, the clarity of intention is there.

This is the place where you become one with the "divine" or "higher self" and connect. The silence comes after the other more chaotic energies of the "monkey mind" are released. This release creates the space to bring you to that place of opening your heart center.

And that is how you ultimately create change in yourself and the world. Your voice is a gift to be cultivated and heard and it starts by getting quiet, identifying the blocks and listening.

But looking within requires courage. And often you may have fear about looking into those hidden crevices and places you have done a good job ignoring thus far.

Now is your chance to take a deeper look in a safe place.

At the end of the chapter I've added a meditation exercise that will guide you through quieting the monkey mind. But now let's look at some other skills you will need to develop before getting to silence.

CULTIVATING COURAGE

As I often say to clients, Courage does not mean that you don't have fear.

In fact, it is quite the opposite.

It means that even though you feel fear, you do it anyways.

A few years ago my maternal grandmother gave me the book *Do It Anyway* by Kent M. Keith. A simple book with clear intentions, it gives a very strong message that whatever you are faced with in life, listen to your heart and move past fear to "do it anyway."

Think of any challenging places in your life that could use your heart energy right now. I welcome you to set your intentions around that space and, though you may be afraid to look deeper, do it anyway!

SETTING YOUR INTENTIONS

Why is setting intentions so important?

Intentions are the key to reconnecting with latent parts of your inner self. The first step is to understand what your intentions are underneath your actions, and then identify what is working and what isn't. You may identify underlying emotional intentions or intentions based on your wounding rather than empowerment. You might even identify some that you are not aware of. Once you understand both your conscious and unconscious intentions when interacting with anyone, and especially yourself, you can really speak from your own inner truth.

An example of this is if you have an inherent intention of pleasing your parents above listening to your own needs. You may be aware of your need to please your parents, however the subconscious part of this intention could be affecting your major life decisions in ways that mirror their path rather than yours.

Once you become aware of this, you can make a choice to shift this intention to pleasing yourself and tending to your own dreams first.

Through becoming crystal clear and heart-centered with your intentions from the inside out, your courage will also increase and you will share yourself from a centered and grounded place. You will then be able to act from a place of clarity in all of your relationships, including with your parents.

The words we speak both out loud and in our heads communicate our intentions to ourselves and to the universe. The clearer you are, the more effective your communication with others will become.

Clear Intention = Clear Communication.

Intimately knowing your intentions and reaching a place of clarity is a process that requires discipline. It takes work and digging, going deep and exploring the wealth of your human emotion, and ultimately taking 100% responsibility for your own healing and for what shows up in your life.

It's about uncovering the reasons why you have not been singing to begin with and peeling away whatever is holding you back.

HOW INTENTIONS MANIFEST

My mother used to sing. She told fun stories that involved staying up all hours of the night singing with friends at work conventions for my father's industry (likely with the aid of liquor). One of those nights though she said something in her voice cracked. From that point forward she completely stopped singing. I suspect that crack had much more to do with her internal state, rather than the state of her physical voice.

Her initial intentions with singing – to simply have fun and share with friends –shut down completely. I will never know exactly what happened to her, though the timing of that convention and when she said I had a "child's voice" (as I mentioned earlier) do coincide.

Her intention then was to save me from pain, however she was projecting her own pain and disappointment onto me without awareness. Rather than letting me have the joy through singing that echoed her own original intention with sharing her voice, she unconsciously took away my joy. And as a result, her joy shut down too.

This is what can happen when intentions are unconscious or not fully realized. The intentions you set, create and change are powerful and affect others. Get clear on what's inside you, bring unconscious intentions to life, set conscious intentions and notice how much things around you begin to change.

GLIMPSES OF BLISS AS A REMINDER

The process of healing can be arduous and painful. It takes a tremendous amount of work and conviction. And it's rarely blissful. But occasionally, bliss happens. It's important to see these moments as barometers of progress rather than a continued state of being.

I remember the first time I felt complete bliss in my own spiritual process. This experience turned into a cycle of moving higher into a state of ecstasy, followed by a period of clearing. In turn, the clearing brought challenges dealing with the next layer of my internal healing and letting go of things that no longer served me.

The onion peels came off one by one, with each peel taking me to a new level of exploration and understanding, giving me a new tool, a new gift to share and a new way to help people. But the process also included letting go of a growing career, many friendships and relationships attached to that life and facing a deep fear around finances and the unknown. And in my experience, when you take the plunge to embark on a spiritual journey, life throws many curve balls your way.

The death of the ego begins with taking away everything in your life that once defined you. In this process you will experience flashes and moments of bliss, so allow them when they come. However, try not to attach yourself to these states of being as they are simply there to show you what is possible, and serve as guideposts along your journey.

And in the rebirth, the reconnection to your voice takes place. And there bliss happens more often.

Do you have any moments of bliss you can recall?

In those moments, how did you feel?

After that feeling passed, what did you experience?

LISTENING TO THE SIGNS AND CONFIRMATION

Along the path of cultivating courage and clarity of intention along with the flashes of bliss, there will be signs. You might believe that life is a series of random events, however I challenge you to look closely at your life, as there are likely guideposts along the way that showed clarity on your path, even at times when you were not listening.

I have often looked for signs and symbols to confirm that I am on the right path, headed in the right direction. And with more silences, cultivated listening and clarity, I am also more open to seeing them. So I tend to see them often.

As I was finishing up the final edits for this book, I was working in a café in Santa Monica on the patio. Deep into the section about the power of your words, part of a tree branch hit me on the head. I looked up and saw that there was a parrot in the tree above me responsible for the incident.

As someone who knows that animals carry symbolism, I looked up "Parrot Medicine", which basically means the energy that this animal is said to embody. I came across the website Universe of Symbolism that described Parrot as "symbolic of truth telling ... speaking from the center of your heart. As Parrot speaks back to you the words you have spoken, you hear your words with no filter. This is a powerful reflection of self, as you are able to recognize the truth of your own words and what you are communicating."

For me, this was confirmation that what I was writing was true to myself. And I saw this as a guidepost confirming that I am on the right path, headed in the right direction.

In looking at your life direction:

What guideposts have shown up in your life so far?

When you think back on the past, can you remember any times when you saw or experienced déjà vu?

Have you ever asked for a sign to confirm something in your life, and you received one?

LETTING YOUR PATH UNFOLD

The pinnacle moment of change for me was after I was fired from my job in orchestra management in Minnesota, as I mentioned earlier. Six months in, I took a vacation to a transformative retreat working with a shaman in the jungle of Peru and returned in a state of elation. This elated state quickly subsided when I was invited into my boss's large stodgy office and she relayed the news that I was being let go.

The phrase "Minnesota nice" rang in my ears as my diminutive female boss, who consistently told me how valuable I was and how much my artistic ideas carried merit, handed me my pink slip.

In one of the many emotional post-firing moments, a coworker forwarded me a poem by Mary Oliver called *The Journey* that encapsulated what I was going through, my knowing I needed to leave and jump off the cliff into the unknown, even though I was petrified and unable to see the forest through the trees.

"One day you finally knew

what you had to do, and began,

though the voices around you

kept shouting

their bad advice –

....

You knew what you had to do"

-excerpt from Mary Oliver's *The Journey*

In Peru, my internal voices were clear that I was in the wrong job, but my head tried to rationalize what was true in my heart. I silenced my voice, so spirit helped me take a leap by handing me that pink slip. What felt like a huge blow to my ego was my gift in disguise: I knew I needed change and lacked the conviction and courage to do so. But luckily, the universe sent me a big kick in the ass and I had no choice but to move forward with my life.

What came next for me was scary, exhilarating, amazing, painful, sad, blissful and, most of all, healing. I developed the tools and wherewithal to heal myself so I could go on to help heal others.

And singing was a big part of this process.

Can you remember your own kick-in-the-ass moments?

Along your own path, when did you realize you were denying your own inner voice?

What life events happened that made you realize it's time to change course?

FROM SILENCE TO SINGING

The most important thing to note is that during the entire three years I worked in orchestral management, I did not sing.

And my soul was hurting.

The one exception was a Kundalini Yoga workshop I took at the old Golden Bridge studio in Hollywood. I was singing the mantra and the person next to me told me that I had a beautiful voice.

Rather than respond with graciousness, I ignored her as I only felt anger – my internal voices screamed, "How dare you compliment my gift that I'm currently ignoring at this point in my life!"

I was resisting my inner knowing that to sing was to heal. I was ignoring the fact that having a job that demanded I prioritize the organization above personal growth and healing made me miserable. It was a reminder that I was out of balance and needed to sing again.

Many months later, my first attempt to sing in public again was at a close friend's wedding in New York, a special event filled with a number of past classical music industry friends. I was asked to sing "Simple Gifts", an Appalachian folk song arranged by Aaron Copland, and I did.

After not singing in front of people for three years, I was scared, recognized my instrument was out of shape, but sang anyways. Though I know in that moment that fear came through my voice rather than joy and I was internally beating myself up about it. My intention was to do something meaningful for my friends.

My friend Ralph made me feel better by simply coming up and telling me I did great. He knew what I had been through and when I saw him and heard his words, I knew he was acknowledging that I did the best I could in that moment.

My voice wasn't quite ready to unleash to the world, but the process had started. My insecurity was there in full force, but I knew I had to get back to that part of myself and sing anyways.

Can you create opportunities to share your voice even if you don't feel ready?

Are there internal voices that want you to share?

Where can you let the path of your voice have more space to unfold?

I HAD A DREAM BUT MY VOICE HAD OTHER PLANS

I came back to Los Angeles with a dream of singing that matched my administrative life. I took voice lessons to get back in shape, practiced every day, sang a few paid gigs for contemporary music concerts and took a few auditions.

Again, my fears came to the surface and I didn't sing so well in the first audition. The second audition I focused more on connecting my voice with my heart rather than on perfection, letting go of my attachment to the outcome, and sang well.

The reconnection with the classical side of my voice and singing was necessary, though after pursuing that route, I realized that I wanted to sing in a way that connected more to the healing side of who I had become.

This is exactly the point where I started writing my own songs again, and improvising on the piano as a practice.

My dreams of living as a classical singer had evolved.

I wanted to be a singer without the classical label.

So I went back to focusing on my other healing business endeavors and continued to sing on my own terms.

My voice no longer wanted the confines of the classical music world. It wanted to be unrestrained and let loose. But I was so blocked and fearful emotionally that I had no idea how to get there. It took another couple of years, but once I accessed the more raw parts of my voice through improvising, I reconnected with the path of my own instrument.

Once you become more comfortable singing again, you should be open to how your voice evolves. The path and dream you once envisioned may have changed. Be open to whatever lies underneath the surface and wants to be expressed through your song.

HOW TO KNOW YOURSELF MORE DEEPLY

In my personal heart-opening journey, self-love was a key component that took me many years to understand. In my case, I did not have the best role models for self-love. I watched people around me blame others for their perceived inadequacies and continued to perpetuate that story myself.

Through exercises, healing explorations, writing, singing and breathing I developed skills to change this learned pattern. One of the tools I found very useful as I moved along in my process was the Brain Dump. As I went into those loud insecure voices and heard their anger and frustration and nearly paralyzing fear, I was able to talk to them and let them be heard by getting them out on paper.

Write, speak, or even sing your frustrations out into the universe and let them be heard. Whether they are rational or irrational, truth or fiction, the voices are there because they need an outlet, a way to get the energy out of the system.

When I brain dumped my insecure feelings and frustrations onto the page and out through my voice, I noticed the energy moved quicker and more easily, allowing more space for the confident energy to come through.

Knowing who you are internally and externally is the most important piece of the puzzle in speaking and living your authentic truth, and in using your voice to communicate with and uplift others. An intimate knowing and unfolding of the light and the dark, things you like and don't like about yourself, and loving every part of it (even the gnarly bits) is necessary for healing. Once you know yourself this intimately, it is only natural that you align with your divine purpose and voice.

ACCESS YOUR PERSONAL POWER THROUGH THE BREATH

Knowing yourself also comes with connection to your personal power, easily accessed through the Diaphragmatic Breath, the most basic tool for singing and living a heart centered life. This power center is literally the midpoint or nucleus of our body and is where the diaphragm resides.

Through this breath, you will learn how to engage that muscle and expand lung capacity to allow the full resonant chamber of the voice to be heard.

As you engage the muscles that control your breath, you take your power back and become much more focused and able to create change in your life. This will help you with intentions and finding your moments of personal bliss by adding power behind your words and vocal delivery.

The power of your voice increases and the power of your body and breath grows, allowing you to become a beacon of creation within your life.

I CAN GUIDE YOU BUT I CAN'T FIX YOU

This book is a guide from which you can develop a personal practice. It is up to you to cultivate the discipline and to show up every day to develop your tools. You must do the work.

Even if you go to see a healer or you work with a life coach, counselor or therapist regularly, you are still the one who needs to show up and do the hard work of healing and growing. They are called "growing pains" for a reason.

Every now and again I have a client that comes to me because that person wants an instant fix and puts me on a pedestal as the person who will save them.

This doesn't work.

I can hold the space for people to heal themselves, but I cannot heal them. It is a 100/100 proposition and the person receiving the healing has to be ready for the growing pains and to work. To help this process, I often give homework in the form of exercises, meditation, mantra and other practices.

The best example to demonstrate how the healing process works is to compare it to growing up as a musician.

When studying an instrument, you usually have only one hour a week with your teacher. The rest of the hours of the week (up to four hours a day or more) you have to develop your own habits and discipline to learn music and to improve while practicing.

The teacher and mentor is a guide, a space holder, someone to help push you. You are the one who puts in the time and effort. Without that level of discipline and practice, you will never be able to transform the lessons and learn.

The actual process of growth and development must be internalized within yourself.

As an example of a quick-fix intention that doesn't work, I had a client once who read about CranioSacral therapy, found me on the internet and showed up for the session with a long-term headache. His intention was to heal the headache.

I asked how long he had that headache and he answered, "15 years!"

Now that's a long time to have chronic pain and no matter what treatment he sought out, Western or otherwise, nothing was going to be able to cure him in an hour.

As I began working with him and his energy, it was clear that he had no idea how to let go or how to let his brain and thoughts relax. I could even see that he was fighting against anything I was doing and in resistance to the release that would actually help his headache get better.

When mentioning to him that this would take some time to heal, he got frustrated. He wanted to heal now and I couldn't help him with that.

And because he didn't get an instant fix, he never came back.

That reaction is a learned response for many people in our fast-food society and social media savvy world. Instant gratification is expected. But if you want to heal and use your voice, you need to be patient and willing to do the work necessary to get there.

Set your intentions, pay attention to the signs, be open to the path unfolding differently than you imagine, use your breath and know that you are the one who houses all the power within you to change. With persistence, patience and discipline, you will.

THE SINGING TOOLBOX

THE BRAIN DUMP

The Brain Dump is a chance for us to air things out and get clarity.

Step 1. Get out a journal or some paper.

Step 2. Start writing anything that comes to mind. Write down the words that are overwhelming and anything that you feel you haven't expressed to people in your life yet. You can also just vent. When you're angry, frustrated, sad or anxiety-ridden, or excited, happy or elated, it helps to write it all down on paper.

Step 3. If thoughts are coming up that you don't like, you can write them down, type them and later tear them up if you want to.

Step 4. In any moment you feel called, and especially when your mind is swimming with thoughts and feelings, write down everything that is in your head that wants to be heard, that wants to be put down on paper. Just get it out. Try not to judge what's coming out, just write or sing the feelings – this is also a useful tool. It should feel good and cathartic and raw.

Step 5. Take a moment to breathe. Notice if you feel like you have more space in your head and more clarity about your next intention.

This is a great exercise to get the thoughts out of your head so you have more clarity and room for creation. As you use this exercise over time you will begin to develop a deeper friendship with yourself, and you'll deepen your understanding of the phrase "know thyself".

DIAPHRAGMATIC BREATHING – The access to your Personal Power Center

Learning how to breathe using your diaphragm gets you to the heart connecting with your full voice.

Diaphragmatic Breathing is effectively using your diaphragm to control *the amount* of breath you use with your voice. The diaphragm is a muscle that lies at the bottom of the ribcage and separates the chest from the abdomen. When you breathe in, the lungs expand and the diaphragm expands downwards; when you breathe out, the lungs collapse and the diaphragm moves upwards.

One of the easiest exercises to learn to use this muscle is the hissing breath.

Step 1. Place your right hand just beneath your sternum and breathe in to the count of 3.

Step 2. Exhale using an "s" hissing noise and, at the same time you do that, push your stomach into your hand. This may feel counterintuitive to exhale and push out at the same time but you will get used to it over time. You can also practice this laying on the floor with your knees bent and feet on the ground. Place a heavy book on top of your stomach. When you exhale on the "s" push into the book at the same time.

Step 3. Repeat this exercise for 3-5 minutes a day. If you feel frustrated or like it's not working, then take a break and come back to it. You are training a muscle and, like any type of exercise, the proper muscle firing takes time to develop properly.

Step 4. If you've never done this before, it will feel counterintuitive, so it might take a while to get the hang of it. Visit my website (www.sacralsounds.com/breathing) for a video illustration of this.

This is the first step in connecting your voice with your breath. Learning to control this muscle opens up the entire vocal mechanism and controls breath flow. Make sure when you practice this that your neck and shoulders are relaxed. It will get easier, I promise.

Finding your power center through this type of exercise is the most important part of accessing your core and getting out of our own way.

And it is the basic tool for preparing to sing!

Chapter 4 – The Mirror Questions and Internalized Voices

How the Voices in our Heads Reflect Our Lives

"The world is a looking glass and gives back to every man the reflection of his own face."
-William Makepeace Thackeray

MIRROR QUESTIONS

"I'm good enough, I'm smart enough, and doggone it people like me!"

The mirror dialogue is often the butt of bad jokes in the new age lexicon. For those of you that remember *Saturday Night Live's* character Stuart Smalley, he encapsulates the positive mirror affirmations in a way that makes them seem ridiculous. However, there is a deep truth in that sketch, as what we tell ourselves is what we become.

Take a moment to look at your own reflection and ask yourself:

What internal dialogue do you have when you look in the mirror?

Are the voices loving and kind?

Or are the voices mean and judgmental?

At times my own voices are annoying and critical, begging for answers seeped in self-sabotage:

Do you really think you are good enough?

Why haven't you exercised more this week?

What makes you think your voice is meant to be heard?

The nasty voices with insecure themes that sometimes scream at me when I look at my reflection echo these words. This constant inner dialogue not only compares me with every single person I come across, but beats down my sense of self-worth, bit by bit.

These voices used to be very loud, but now are mostly silent even though they creep in from time to time. The silence comes only when those voices are looked at, heard and actively quieted with a gentle, yet assertive internal force. And in my case, it took some work.

Over time I realized that these voices were often not my own. They were echoing the voices of my parents, friends, colleagues, mentors, enemies, society and extended family members. They were voices of others who infiltrated my very existence and drowned out the things I knew to be true. And the voices also created belief systems based on the actions or inactions of the people around me. With others' voices being so loud, it was very difficult to hear, let alone trust, the deepest internal voice that was mine.

Each stage of healing brings more of these voices to the surface. Every time I let go of an old shell, an old paradigm of who I was, I find some of the old voices come back to the surface and I have to work through them again.

Though with each breakthrough and jumping off point, I find I am able to calm them down more quickly with tools I've developed and an innate sense of knowing which voices are real and which voices are simple self-sabotage.

At the moment I began to know my own worth and talk and sing my truth from this space of clarity, everything in my life changed. And so will yours.

So how do you identify and learn to quiet those voices and develop the tools to decipher and discern their usefulness?

First, by identifying the origin of each voice.

Start by paying attention to all of the voices you hear in your internal dialogue and then begin to really listen and identify who the voices you are hearing belong to.

Is that voice male or female?

Is it loud or soft?

Is it helpful or unhelpful?

By knowing whose voice is coloring the content, and then breaking each one down, you can identify which voice is yours. Then you begin to let your inner truth speak louder than the externally derived voices.

Once you are able to quiet the harsh voices and give yourself validation through your own words and acknowledgment, you will no longer need validation from others. It all starts with changing the way you speak to yourself.

The negative voices might still be there, but they will eventually quiet down and fade into the background.

How do you begin the journey to get there?

The easiest way is to break down the voices into positive and negative aspects. Identify both negative criticism and constructive criticism, and then recognize the internal belief systems that have developed in you as a result of each voice.

From that place of complete awareness, you can begin to shift the voices, talk to them differently and know better when to listen and act on them and when to push through and let them fade.

In order to illustrate these various voices and give you a deeper understanding of how they can manifest, I will share some of my own identification with the voices that shaped my journey.

THE CREATIVE MIND AND THE VOICES UNDERNEATH

Every singer, artist, performer, writer or speaker I know deals with internal critical voices. It is, in fact, a part of being a creative artist. Putting yourself out there takes courage and guts and the questioning is an important, healthy part of the creative process. However, the self-sabotage voices, if not dealt with in a healthy way, can render you numb and ineffectual.

When you choose the path of a performer or any path in the public eye, you must be ready to listen to many critics. Whenever you put yourself out there in any capacity, people will come forth with varying opinions. And you must learn to decipher between the constructive criticism and the criticism coming from those who are destructive.

As a wise gypsy healer once told me, "No matter what you do in this life, 1/3 of the people you come in contact with will love it, 1/3 of the people will hate it, and the other 1/3 won't give a S@#t! So focus on those who love it and don't worry about the rest!"

In my experience, those who have been the most critical and vocal are usually the ones who are actually projecting their own fears. Their words are coming from a place of self-doubt, fear and scarcity. But the ones who can be challenging while offering constructive criticism, meaning they come from the intention of truly wanting you to become better, are the ones to learn from.

So how do the negative voices manifest, and how do you differentiate the two?

Let me explain how they manifested for me.

I housed the critical voices deep in my psyche. Each person who told me what was wrong with my piano playing stuck like glue since the focus was so much on what was wrong. And they also became my own voices. Rather than develop confidence in my own playing or singing, these more destructive voices would talk to me during a performance. The loud voices who yelled that I wasn't good enough

46

and never would be taken seriously as a performer looped on repeat.

So I was often in my head. Rather than having the experience of raising an audience into joy and sharing the music in a loving state, I was embodying my insecurities, which never felt good. And it showed.

Once, when I was studying piano in Amsterdam, my boyfriend at the time listened to me play one evening and observed that my playing sounded like I hated music. At that time, he was right. My internal voices were not about creating an experience, they were about practicing so as not to make a mistake, and there is no joy in embodying fear about making mistakes.

I eventually learned that he was offering an honest experience of my playing and what I was communicating underneath it all. It wasn't easy to hear his words and they stuck with me. So I internalized what he said and it carried through many years. In retrospect I know he spoke the truth in the moment, though I did not have the tools to know these voices could be changed.

I eventually flipped those perfectionist voices into the joyful heart space and realized that it is possible to turn all of the voices we don't like into things that can help. Now, thankfully, I am in the joy space most of the time when creating music.

You can also learn how to do this step-by-step through continuing this internal voice identification process.

NEGATIVE VOICES AND CRITICISM

THE VOICE OF A TEACHER

One summer while I was in high school as a student, I attended a well-known music festival and had a male piano teacher who sat me down at a lesson with a list of all the reasons I should not become a classical pianist written on a yellow notepad. I remember his words well:

"You are too social.

You are too pretty.

Your clothes are too nice.

You should really major in something else rather than music."

At 17, with my main aspiration being the piano, I was devastated.

To be fair to the teacher, it's important to set the stage.

The night before this fateful piano "lesson", I was playing a Brahms Capriccio in a recital and I had overwhelming performance anxiety. It was my first performance of the summer and the internal negative voices were screaming.

The overwhelm manifested as a meltdown about my shoes, in the performance hall, in front of the arriving audience – which is clearly what the teacher was basing his assessment on.

I was a female teenager obsessed with my appearance and hadn't seen good examples of what to do with those overwhelming feelings. So I transferred them into something else – in this case it was my shoes. And clearly, I had an issue with anxiety.

It is a common human behavior to have pent up feelings and then unleash them about something seemingly small that has nothing to do with the actual issue. Though my family, this teacher and I did not have tools to deal with this behavior back then.

And what I really needed was a mentor to help me understand and change my behavior and relationship within myself. Someone to reflect back to me what they saw and help me see that I was simply not expressing the truth of what I was feeling.

Instead I felt attacked. And that teacher's list had nothing to do with the real issue of dealing with severe performance anxiety.

Even though I went on to major in piano and continue that path regardless of his discouragement, his voice stuck with me as a belief that if I was an attractive person then I could never be really gifted at playing the piano and dedicating myself to a musician's life.

In drawing upon the phrase from the previous chapter of *Do it Anyway* I kept feeding my piano dreams. That same year I thankfully found a wonderful teacher at the University of North Carolina in Greensboro who helped me prepare for college auditions.

One day, the dream-crushing teacher came to teach a masterclass and my current teacher (who did not know about the yellow notepad) asked if I wanted to play something since we'd worked together before.

Well, that was just the opportunity I needed to prove my worth and begin to quiet the loud voices.

I actually played better in that masterclass than I had ever played in my life up until that point, in a performance of Debussy's *Minstrels* Prelude.

He was impressed and I felt validated.

Even after this experience, I continued to fight the voices for years and they still lingered as reminders of someone else's perception entering and affecting my own.

They were not my beliefs, but they reflected his bias and misogyny.

And often I came back to these places again to fight them, look at them and conquer them. The sticky voices came unglued in multiple stages and only as a result of stark determination.

You will also learn to do the same.

THE VOICES OF MY MOTHER AND FATHER

A mother's voice is heard from the womb and you internalize everything she says, does and feels as you develop. Once you leave the womb, the nurturing bond you develop with your mom is very

49

important. If you have a good nurturing bond, the relationship is strong, and if you don't have that nurturing bond, there is a part of you that will always continue to search for it.

With my own mother we never bonded that way. We came from completely opposite ends of the spectrum in terms of our interests, perceptions of people and life, and we rarely agreed on anything. As I got older, though, I realized that some of her behaviors, especially in terms of being reactive to people and situations, were deeply embedded in my being too.

The voice I internalized from my mother was the way she spoke to me, and also to herself: unkind, critical and judgmental. And that voice was loud for most of my life.

I was not able to appreciate or take in any of the success I had achieved because I didn't know how to let it in or receive it. I wanted to hear her kind words of support and encouragement, however she was only capable of showing love by giving material gifts. Because I longed to hear more words of emotional support and encouragement and never got what I desired, I searched to fulfill that need by seeking outside approval in my work and personal life.

Meanwhile, her internalized critical voices were always at play, and it took me years to learn to be nice to myself and to identify the negative voices and quiet them. This required looking at the parts of myself that I didn't like, which were similar to her, and changing those thought patterns and behaviors. I took responsibility for my own perpetuation of ingrained patterns and voices by identifying and changing them from victim to survivor to transformer.

While my mother's voice still loomed large in my psyche, I developed a narcissism that reflected hers and I made all stories about me. I took everything personally.

Once at dinner with my youngest brother in New York, he flat out interrupted the conversation about our parents' problems with, "It's not always about you!"

I was rendered speechless.

It cut deep, but he was right.

The nine-year-old child inside me who cried in a corner when her parents were fighting was still blaming herself years later. And I was still making it about me, rather than seeing the deeper truths that my parents' relationship issues were between them.

Understanding the origin of your perceptions and healing them changes your ability to develop as a compassionate human. As your compassion grows and you deal with the critical voices in your own head, then you can sing and communicate from a place of wholeness and awareness, rather than wounding.

In your life, where have you internalized an external situation and made it about you?

What stories are you telling yourself that stemmed from a close relative?

Are you ready to change those stories?

My father's voice also showed up both in my conscious and unconscious life.

My relationship with my father was much easier than that with my mother. However, even though the primary voice from him was positive, I also housed subconscious negative voices from his long periods of absence. As a traveling businessman, he was away from home more than half of the year. It took many years to realize that his absence caused me pain. I shoved it down and concentrated on school and work, developing classic workaholic behaviors modeled on his own (another mirrored reflection).

His voice was encouraging to a point, though the quieter voices had me believe that men were meant to be gone, supportive only when convenient and always made work their first priority. He also tuned out my mother's voice, and eventually my brothers' and my voice too, so we all felt unheard by him.

51

This perception of men showed up in all of my relationships – I chose men who were workaholics, lived in other cities and never listened to me. However, once I cultivated my awareness, I understood that my father's decisions were based in his own wounding and not mine.

I ultimately turned those voices into positive manifestations by making a concerted effort to face my internal fears and issues head on. I realized those voices were not truth and only stemmed from the example set for me. I developed a more positive internal dialogue about men.

And my relationships have deepened as a result.

To shift the perspective, there were also positive voices from my parents that ultimately became an important part of my empowered inner dialogue.

My mother taught me to respect all people regardless of color, race or sexual preference. Her voice was always clear that all people should be treated with respect, period. And my father shared that voice.

As far as my father goes, I know his ultimate wish was for me to be happy. He never tried to change my desires or dreams, even when they were unconventional. His voice was always encouraging, even if he didn't understand me. The best example of this was when I was in my early 20s. I distinctly remember feeling the pressure from others regarding relationships and facing judgment because I was single with no current prospects on the horizon.

He was very supportive and thoughtful with his response and said with conviction, "I don't care if you ever get married, I just want you to be happy!"

I carry that voice with me always.

That intention was clear.

What intentions from others in your childhood do you feel might be buried in your subconscious?

Where do you struggle in your life at present and can you look at where those old intentions and beliefs might be buried?

Is there anyone in your life you feel simply wants you to be happy?

THE VOICE OF THY SELF AND LEARNING TO LISTEN

For many years I was a terrible listener to both my own voice and to others' voices, except those negative ones that seemed to color my experience of the world. I wasn't always able to hear people when they shared this with me, whether kindly or critically.

Since I grew up feeling unheard and misunderstood, I was constantly seeking out this feeling and didn't have the tools at the time to express this in a healthy way. Through my journey in the healing arts and deep friendships that held space for me to grow, I was able to identify this deep need to be heard, address it and shift it. I had to change my own behavior to move into a space of asking more questions, being more present, and learning to quiet my own internal voices while another was speaking.

This also helped with my expression through singing. The more I was able to listen to others and myself, learn from constructive criticism and grow, the more I could apply these openings to my voice. My words became stronger and my ears more acute. I learned how to be present with my singing voice and experience a state where I became fully immersed in singing and eventually more present in all of my interactions with people.

As a healer by profession, holding space for others through listening is one of the primary functions of the job. I spend hours doing this, and at the end of the day I sometimes want to unload and talk about my own stuff. My listening capacity is tapped out.

This can be daunting for the person on the other side of the friendship or relationship.

I love holding space and I also love good conversation, however, when I am tapped out, I sometimes shut down. With active awareness of this pattern within myself, I could shift this to create more balance with sharing in my relationships. Awareness creates balance and the voice can find its own expression internally to project the emotions externally from this place.

Sometimes I was a really good listener and sometimes I wasn't. Though the truth was that the people who were most vocal about what they saw in me were also sometimes good listeners and sometimes not.

We all reflect the good and bad in each other and all relationships take work, good communication and willingness from both parties to grow. Some friendships and relationships are meant to come in for a short time and others are meant to last through the challenges. As you grow and others in your life grow, balance comes more easily.

I finally came to understand that the mirror extends outwards from the self. Everything you see in your life is a reflection of who you are and where you are. No other person sees the world exactly the same way you do, and your perception of what you see defines your very existence. How you respond to every experience you've had shapes this. Once you understand that everyone around you reflects your own inner state of being, beginning with how you see and talk to yourself, you can see how you can change your existence just by changing your mirror dialogue.

THE VOICES OF *A BEAUTIFUL MIND*

In my private client sessions I often refer to the movie *A Beautiful Mind* to illustrate how you can deal with these voices.

In the movie, the main character suffers from schizophrenia and it manifests as characters or hallucinations. Over time, when he decides to give up his medication (because it shuts down his cognitive skills and sex drive) he learns how to live with the voices and they are eventually characters seen in the distance on a park bench practicing silence.

He learned how to first listen to the voices and then to eventually quiet them. He began to listen to his own internal voice above all others. The voices never completely went away, but they were relegated to stillness and no longer had any control over his actions.

Healing with your voice begins with listening to the inner voices even more deeply than before so you can relegate the unwanted ones to the park bench in the background in silence.

HOW TO HANDLE CONFLICT THROUGH OTHERS' NEGATIVE VOICES

One of my favorite books about effectively using your words is *Nonviolent Communication* by Marshall Rosenberg. His primary message is that, when conflict arises in interactions with people and you are experiencing intense reactions, chances are that the other person is not feeling heard. Once you take the time to listen and that other person feels heard, conflict often diffuses.

And your internal negative voices also need to be heard in order to change and be calmed.

People who react strongly and create conflict are often trying to be heard by anyone and everyone, but they never quite feel people meet them in that place. If you are experiencing these same feelings within yourself, you can learn to master listening to your own feelings and express them in a healthy way. You can learn to be your own best listener and, in turn, become a better listener to others.

Cultivating the reactive voices within yourself will help you when coming in contact with them.

Who do you experience conflict with in your daily life?

Do you feel that person feels heard?

Do you think there is a way you can become a better listener to that person?

POSITIVE VOICES AND CONSTRUCTIVE CRITICISM

THE VOICE OF A MENTOR

This book existed in my head for a couple of years before I finally began writing. The process finally gelled when I decided to write the book under the tutelage of Angela Lauria, creator of *The Author Incubator*. As a new mentor, Angela took me on a journey I wasn't expecting.

In the process, I completely resisted owning one of the primary things that I am:

A singer.

Now, that seems strange given the title and premise of the book, my life history studying voice and piano and performing throughout most of my life.

But somewhere in me, there was a voice that spoke loudly telling me that I wasn't really good enough – STILL!

When I started writing this book, I found myself in that deep place of insecurity again, questioning who I was to be teaching other people about singing. Somehow, the insecure parts believed in the negative voices that kept saying I wasn't good enough to put myself out there and, heavens, what would people think?

But these voices were not the truth.

I finally started to listen to the voices that told me that my purpose was to help people connect with their voice through sharing how I did the same. I spoke before about how my voice opened up when I did my sound healing training in San Francisco.

And everyone responded. I know that my healing abilities gifted from the divine resided in my voice, but I had to get through all of those negative voices to be able to really own that part of myself.

And what I learned from Angela was how important it is to really own your gifts and who you are. Now I own my gifts in a more profound way than I ever have, seeing my reflection as a healer who shares my voice and process with others and whose life purpose is to help those who are ready to unlock their own vocal potential.

The mirrored reflection continues to change through a commitment to constant awareness and the ability to change my internal dialogue. This all happens through continuing to cultivate my practice and my voice.

Who are the positive mentors in your life?

Are there any practitioners, healers or counselors that you rely on for reflection?

Do you have people in your life capable of pushing you to be your best self?

FAMILY VOICES THAT SUPPORT

Of all of my extended family, there is one person I connect with deeply in terms of shared interests and common ways of looking at the world and that is my cousin Katy, who is both my goddaughter and friend. She also gifted me the honor of officiating her wedding.

I am grateful I have one person in my extended family that shares my voice and also hears mine on the same level. Having her has been pivotal in getting to where I am now with my life. Her voice often reflects my own and those positive reflections from her have helped my confidence levels in recent years.

She's the voice I relish and carry when I need someone to listen completely without judgment. She knows me intimately and she will tell me the truth. That I can count on.

Do you have anyone in your life who reflects your shared interests?

What voices reflect the interests you hold most sacred?

Can you identify the person or people you can call when you really need someone to just hold space for you and listen?

LEARNING TO LISTEN TO YOUR OWN VOICE ABOVE OTHERS

As a single person for most of my life, friends often took the place of family for me. And, being an unusual person, my friends also understood me more than my parents did.

However, I often relied on the opinions of friends and the occasional significant others as truths, negating my own inner opinions in favor of being pleasing and accommodating. I did not realize I was shutting my voice down and allowing their voices to become louder than my own.

I desperately wanted to fit in so I took in every word people said to me and tried to be what everyone else might like or whom that person thought I should be rather than simply being myself.

Both my mother and my friends would give me dating advice and told me that I needed to create an aura of mystery about myself. They inferred that there was something wrong with me in terms of how I approached dating and men. Now on some level, they were right in terms of my openness, but a deeper part of me couldn't make sense of this logic.

So basically I was supposed to pretend to be someone I wasn't, in order to get someone to "love me" and want to be with me, get married and then spring on them who I really am?

To me, that sounded like a surefire recipe for divorce and misery.

But I listened to them and tried to take that advice that led me through many failed dating experiences and drawing in men who reflected the same insecurities I was having. At the moment I said f**k it and decided to just be myself, my dating experiences improved immensely and, even when things didn't work, the communication and way of relating felt healthy and connected.

I followed my own inner compass, learned how to be vulnerable and finally developed the confidence to be myself.

Thank God.

It was finally safe to listen to myself.

And to just be me.

When and where do you find it hard to be yourself?

Do you have people in your life who always tell you to be or act differently than in ways that are true to yourself?

How can you listen to your own inner compass more?

As you begin to speak to yourself with compassion, care and kindness, notice how others around you reflect that back to you. Identify the voices, decipher the intention and make a choice to listen to the ones that help you the most. If you are kind to yourself, then no one can really hurt you because you inherently know that is not the mirrored container that you hold.

With your outward voice, it's important that you learn to do the same. Take advice from others, listen where needed, but ultimately use the mirror to listen to yourself. Your internal voice will guide you on your path without fail.

It's those that go against the grain that create the most amount of change in the world, not those who listen only to the voices of others. And every time you listen and act on your true voice, you become the best version of yourself.

In the words of Mahatma Gandhi, "Be the change you wish to see in the world."

And this begins with the voice.

THE SINGING TOOLBOX

THE MIRRORED REFLECTION AND VOICE IDENTIFICATION

In order to intimately understand the mirror, it is important to know the questions to ask yourself. The mirror can reflect both the positive and negative parts of who you are, so this exercise will help identify the places where you can bring more joy and compassion into your daily life.

Step 1. List 5 people who are important in your life.

Step 2. Write down 3-5 things about each person that you admire, appreciate or respect.

Step 3. Write down 3-5 things you dislike or find challenging about each person.

Step 4. Next to each attribute, both positive and negative, write down how each of those things makes you feel.

Step 5. Now go back and look at your list and write in a third column if this quality is something you also recognize in yourself. If it's something good, know that you can build upon this in your life as something reflecting your inner spirit. If it's something you don't like, just become more aware, note how you can work on that particular thing and begin to practice compassion towards both yourself and that other person.

This type of awareness and reflection through the mirror can be used anytime you have intense emotions on both sides of the spectrum with another person. Everything in your life, and especially your reactions to things, seeks to get your attention and encourages you to look more deeply inward at yourself. And looking through this lens is how you heal, develop more tools and are able to speak and communicate with care, compassion and joy in your relationships. Before long, your singing will begin to reflect this inner work.

Chapter 5 – Bringing the Shadow to Light

Embracing the Darkness as a Tool

"One does not become enlightened by imagining figures of light, but by making the darkness conscious."
– Carl Jung

Lurking in the back of your mind are the dark places, the things you don't like to look at and the things you might want to run away from. All known as: The Shadow.

Horror movies use the shadow as an ominous figure, Peter Pan loses his shadow and later gets it back and many new age gurus talk about shadow work.

But what does that really mean?

The Shadow is medicine of the soul, which takes you into the cocoon to recalibrate before emerging as the butterfly. Knowing and understanding the darker part of yourself, your life and the lives around you actually prepares you to transform. This is necessary in order to hold space for others and clear those parts that hold you back from becoming your best self. Understanding this part of the yin and yang balance is incredibly important in learning to transform and deal with your emotions in a healthy way.

This means getting to know your dark side just as well as your light side and seeing the wisdom in *both.*

In fact, it is the shadow that will often show you the way back into the light. When you allow yourself to feel the dark emotions the shadow presents while sitting with your own inner resistance, often the emotions move more quickly back to equilibrium.

Now the word "shadow" might elicit a fearful response from you because darkness is often pushed away in favor of the light. I invite you to see the shadow as a teaching tool, rather than something to ignore. Feeling the shadow emotions – fear, grief, sadness, anger, irritation, rage – is normal and meant to come up in the growth process.

And as a singer, connecting with the dark is just as important as connecting with the light, experiencing and communicating the yin and the yang. It is how you can access the full range of human emotion and express the dark and light of your soul.

In the previous chapter I shared my process of continuing to perform despite my voices of self-doubt. It's literally how I shined a light on those areas where I felt inadequate and learned how to change them. Through identifying my feelings and doubts about singing, I was better able to identify similar feelings of inadequacy at work, in relationships, at home and while speaking or communicating.

This is something you can cultivate through your voice, as well. You can use your voices of self-doubt to your advantage through awareness and cultivating a different relationship with those voices. And to do that you must first address what lies in your subconscious mind.

LIMITING BELIEFS

Limiting beliefs are subconscious or conscious beliefs that come from your conditioning, traumas or losses that keep you stuck in patterns or old belief systems. Those lurking dark places I mentioned earlier house these beliefs within your psyche. Before we move into the specific shadow emotions, it's important to look at those dark spots and name them.

Most of the time they are unconscious, though sometimes you might be aware of them. For example, you might want to meet your life partner and every time you find someone you sense a connection with, the relationship doesn't work out, again.

You might ask yourself why that keeps happening.

Chances are there is a belief you formed in childhood or adulthood after a trauma that perpetuates the story "I am not worthy of love."

You may or may not be aware that belief is in there.

However, identifying these beliefs and knowing where they come from is the first step in changing them.

A client of mine has spent years following the 12-Step AA Program. She is very clear that her internal limiting belief is "I am not enough." The program helps her deal with that thought by identification, understanding where it came from and then dealing with it whenever it shows up.

Now she sees that belief clearly whenever she comes across a difficult work or relationship situation, and has the ability to work with it and use it as a barometer for her own progress.

For your own subconscious limiting beliefs, you may find they become clearer when going deeper into the dark spots so you can use them. Let's start by looking at the main shadow emotions and tools for working through them.

GRIEF

Grief is a given part of the human experience. It is one of the cycles of human emotion that can break you wide open into new spaces of being, and can also keep you stuck.

At some point you will experience grief and it will affect you deeply. Losing someone close to you can be both a painful and beautiful experience. In my own life, losing my father is what prompted me to start changing my life and doing the work I am doing now. The change took time and I learned how grief is a non-linear process.

Grief is the culmination of many shadow emotions and unresolved questions like:

Anger - How could you go so soon?

Fear - What will I do without you?

Guilt - Was something left unsaid or undone?

Sadness - How will I ever get over missing you?

Grief is not limited to losing people: it can also be grief over leaving a job, a life you've created, a divorce, a major move, a friendship going away or a business failure. Learning how to process the stages of grief in whatever form they take is also part of transformation. With the voice, grief can be very clearly expressed through song. The song *Angel* that I wrote as a reflection of my father's death took me a year to complete because I kept crying as I wrote it. However, using my own voice to express my emotions aided my grieving process and gave me peace.

If my father was still alive, I might still be in my old career helping everyone else create, rather than pursuing my own artistic and healing endeavors. Finding peace in the process, and in going through that part of the shadow, was how I turned things around in my life. And though I miss him, I am grateful for the lessons and the impetus to turn my life around into a place where I am connected to my heart-centered work.

DEPRESSION

Now, writing about my heart work also calls for a confession from my own shadow. I am someone who has suffered from mild depression throughout a good chunk of my life. Through various therapists, trying on medication and varying bits of advice, I learned that for me depression was a learned reaction to the

66

behavior of the people around me rather than my inherent nature. And that it was often a reaction to suppressed anger.

I grew up in a household where truths were unspoken and swept under the rug when questioned. This made me feel crazy. Underneath it all, I was angry because I knew that what I was experiencing wasn't really truth, but I didn't have the tools to express the emotions I was feeling and they got stuck.

That stuckness turned into depression. It was my way of shutting down the external stimulus and retreating.

You may never have suffered from feeling depressed, though I am sure you have come into contact with someone who has. Feeling a bit depressed at times is a normal part of life's ups and downs, but lingering depression is another thing entirely.

I went through much process work to understand the depression deeply, and to transform these feelings into something positive. I now see any depressed feelings as trying to get my attention about something I am not speaking out loud. If I feel depressed, I know I am not expressing something that needs to get out, so I make the effort to have that conversation, move through the stuck energy of procrastination and ask for help if I need it.

In the recent animated movie *Inside Out*, you get insight into the different voices and characters in the head of the main character, Riley. The brilliant story initially focuses on being happy as the primary goal with the character Joy running the show above the other feeling characters. As the story moves on, Riley gets depressed because of her family move and then, sadly, all of her systems shut down. The characters, in an effort to save Riley from complete meltdown, Joy in particular, finally see that sadness is just as necessary for Riley to feel in order to move through her life experience. Speaking about these other feelings gets her back to joy.

All the shadow emotions are necessary to process information.

ANGER

On the flip side of depression lies anger.

Anger was always scary for me and depression covered it up. Now that I'm at a point in my life where I can healthily express something that makes me angry, I no longer feel depressed. And my life is healthier and happier, more creative and flowering.

It happened not by ignoring these feelings but by looking at them, understanding them and expressing them, in the same way Riley did in *Inside Out.*

The external shadow of society – violence, wars, poverty and suffering – is something you face every day dealing with the outside world and that can sometimes be challenging. It is what I refer to as the "shadow outside". You are not in control of external events, though you can begin to shift your internal response to them by focusing on your own "shadow inside" and transforming that energy.

When you notice any anxiety, stress and fear responses in yourself as a reaction to external events, really take some time to sit with your reaction and see if you can transform the feeling within yourself. Rather than letting your thoughts go down the path of thinking that things should be different than they are, worrying about things that have not yet happened and creating your own stress by saying yes to too many things, take a moment to look more deeply into what is happening. Ask yourself how you can shift the feelings within yourself first. There is a reason that you are supposed to put your own oxygen mask on first in an airplane.

Once you have sat with these feelings, see if your reaction to the external events changes. Often what will come up are ways to help your inner shadow that will in turn give you clarity as to how to bring more positive energy into your space. This internal/external way of looking at the shadow is a personal Think Globally, Act Locally way of shifting the energy inside you and extending it outward to your external environment.

FEAR

The current world is in a state where the media is always in your face and often advertising, social media and television play to the energy of fear. Even from an early age I was taught to be fearful of what might happen, even though almost 99% of the time, that "thing" never occurred. I had a deep fear of being alone, of being in uncomfortable situations, of falling in love with the wrong person and an even deeper fear that, when I actually showed people who I was, they would leave. I housed a very deep fear of abandonment.

These fears were reflected in the emotions that came through my voice. I disconnected from these intense feelings and went through the motions rather than fully letting myself feel. It seemed easier to go through the motions than to really take an in-depth look at what I was experiencing. And I got stuck in a cycle of trying to convince my own inner voice that the life I'd created was what I really wanted.

I felt abandoned, though it was really my louder voices abandoning my quieter ones. I had abandoned myself.

While it is normal for human beings to have fears, it is a choice to continue to let fear dictate your life. All of us have things that haunt us sometimes, though most of our fears are really about things that happened in the past or that we are afraid might happen in the future. The feelings themselves are often not warranted in the truth of the moment.

FEAR = False Evidence Appearing Real

This might be one of my most favorite acronyms when working with the shadow.

In 2016 I felt an extraordinary internal urgency to take a sound healing trip to Egypt. It was a bucket list trip and deep down I knew I was destined to be with this carefully curated group at this particular time, even though I didn't know anyone when I signed up.

When I shared my plans with some friends and family members, the first reactions I received were doubts about whether or not I would be safe. And, in truth, it brought up some fears within myself that I needed to look at. Then one night I told someone close to me who had a strong Egyptian connection about my plans. He questioned why I would go to Egypt in the current worldly climate and I found myself accessing my own fearful state of mind. I had my regular bodywork client that evening and she had a deck of divination soul cards.

Compelled to draw one, the card I pulled was DEATH.

In the spiritual sense, a Death card doesn't mean actual human death but rather defines death as a metaphor for the death of a way of being, a major loss, or death of a part of yourself. However, given the timing of that conversation, it indeed felt ominous, and I felt the need to update my advance care directive when I got home later that evening.

So I sat with the feelings. I realized that I didn't have a deep fear of death, however, I did have a fear of living through trauma.

What if I went to Egypt and God forbid there was a terrorist attack? After sitting with it for a day, I realized that if I truly trust in divine timing, then if that was meant to happen, it would. And if something did indeed happen, I had the strength to withstand it.

And I let the fear go to the wind.

I knew internally that it was not my time and that going on the trip was important for me. I'm glad I listened to the internal voices, as I have no regrets. Egypt was the best vacation of my life so far.

This story demonstrates how fear is something to sit with, to look at, to understand and ultimately to decide if it is a warning to be heeded or not.

Pulling that card prompted a soul searching and facilitated the death of my internal fear of something terrible happening to me. I learned and listened.

Fear should be listened to and felt in silence. In this listening it will tell you if the fear is warranted or not. Continuing to cultivate your innate courage will lead you to the other side of conquering what arises. Identify your limiting beliefs, identify the shadow feelings as they surface and give expression to the feelings as they arise. This will open any places that you might be stuck.

In doing this you will become friends with your shadow and be able to use these feelings as fuel for growth and trusting what unfolds along your path.

I personally believe that you are always where you are meant to be at the time you are meant to be there. However, at moments when I forget this core belief and need to curb my own fear and anxiety, I combat the feelings by taking deep breaths and sitting still. In this place I remind myself of the truth: that things are this way in this moment for a reason, even if the reason may not be clear to me yet. In this space, I work though my shadow emotions of grief, depression, anger and fear and transcend them.

The shadow is a tool to be welcomed and embraced. Express gratitude that the shadow can push you to the limits and force you to grow. Instead of trying to slay the shadow and push it away, allow it to push you on the road to self-improvement and truth.

Use it, move it, learn the lessons, sing, dance and carry on!

THE SINGING TOOLBOX

LISTENING TO THE SHADOW

Step 1. Take a moment to set your intention to work with whatever difficulties you are having related to fear, grief, depression, sadness or anxiety.

Step 2. Close your eyes and begin to observe your breath.

Step 3. As you observe your breath, begin to notice any discomfort or pain that arises. Welcome whatever that feeling is to come in at full force.

Step 4. As you breathe, really feel that emotion, breathe into it.

If you feel like crying, allow the release.

If you feel like you want to hit someone, breathe into it or hit a pillow!

If you feel like you are edgy, move your body around in circles emanating from the hips. Start in one direction, then move to the other direction. Do this until the energy dissipates.

Step 5. Close your eyes and notice that there is a movie screen in front of you. Allow any thoughts that arise to transfer to the movie screen. As the thoughts begin to circulate, imagine taking a few steps back from the screen. Then look at the movie screen and the swirling thoughts. Think about your intention and see if anything comes into focus. Just notice what appears and make note. Allow the energy to be there. As you watch what arises, ask the energy what it is trying to teach you. Stay quietly with your breath and allow the space for the answer to arise. Often the clarity and answers will come, giving you the ability to move through and navigate the shadow more easily.

Step 6. Repeat. This exercise sometimes requires multiple visits in order to get the answers. Try your best to be patient with the process and allow the answers to arise in their perfect timing. Persistence will pay off with time and dedication. I promise.

SHAKING MEDICINE

"Shaking Medicine" is a common practice in indigenous cultures to get rid of any unwanted energy. I find it is the quickest and easiest way to move energy in the body and mind when stuck in the shadow emotions. It is also a way to move past procrastination and lethargy.

Step 1. Listen to tracks involving drums. I created my own Shaking Medicine with the "Fire" track from my ELEMENTAL ALCHEMY CD featuring Andre Ripa on drums and Ben Powell on violin. This is a good track to use for this purpose and was created with that intention in mind. (It also comes as a free download with this book.) You can also visit Spotify or any other music service and search for tribal drumming.

Step 2. Close your eyes and let the music move through you, open your voice, let it all out and move your body and sing as if no one is listening.

Step 3. Continue to move and create sound in whatever way feels good and allow the release to happen.

Step 4. When complete after at least 5-10 minutes of shaking, lay down in savasana (corpse pose) for another 5 minutes, allowing the energy to sink in.

6 – Balancing the Body and Mind

Seven Chakras to bring you back into alignment with your voice

*"No person, no place, and no thing has any power over us, for 'we'
are the only thinkers in our mind. When we create peace and
harmony and balance in our minds, we will find it in our lives."*
-Louise L. Hay

Working with the chakras is an effective way for you to use the
energy field within the body to create centered alignment. The
previous chapters have prepared you more deeply to come into this
space through setting intentions, identifying the voices in your
head and working with your shadow. All of the exercises and
practices we discussed thus far have hopefully helped you to access
more clarity in your voice.

Now we will go further into the process of opening by looking at
the current state of your voice. The first step is to look at what is
currently reflected in the flow of energy in your body and mind.
Then you will identify and clear the blocks that are keeping you
from expressing your true voice.

Let's explore the parts of the body that house these energy
centers.

The study of the chakras, first documented in Sanskrit writings
called the Vedas, is said to have originated in India sometime
between 1500BC and 500BC. The idea is that each chakra in the
body houses a different energy and when all seven energy centers
are working at their optimum level the person is at peace and in the
flow of life.

There are seven chakras from top to bottom:

Crown

Third Eye

Throat

Heart

Solar Plexus

Sacral

Root

In this chapter, I will take you through each one in detail. My personal approach is to use the voice, aromatherapy and movement exercises and to give you the tools to do the same. This sequence brings each chakra into alignment.

Much has been written about the chakras and the embodiment of these seven energy centers of the body, and I find that each person's relation to them is an individual experience. My own journey in learning about the chakras began through my yoga practice and yoga teacher training in New York. Later in my spiritual studies, I also studied Polarity Therapy, a type of bodywork that focuses on chakras, the elements and astrology in relation to healing. They have added another dimension to my work and I use them often in working with the voice.

When singing, all seven chakras are activated, opened and aligned by using the diaphragmatic breath. There are also specific tones you can use for each center, which I will share at the end of the chapter. Alignment can also be found through regular meditation and breath exercises.

Similar to identifying the voices that run your life, identifying where you might need more balance in a particular chakra, and knowing how to readjust that chakra, will bring you back into alignment more quickly.

The highest state of chakra alignment is referred to as a Kundalini awakening, a state that can be most easily accessed through its namesake Kundalini Yoga. Yoga is a very effective practice for chakra alignment and I recommend that, as you move through this step of chakra balancing, shop around your local yoga studios to find a class that resonates with you. You can also go online to find a class or visit Gaia.com, a wonderful subscription streaming service that focuses on spiritual content featuring many different yoga classes.

Working with essential oils can also be helpful in balancing in the chakras. I have listed my favorite Young Living™ Essential Oils next to each chakra as suggestions for you to use. However, you can also use any oils that call to you, as the combination of aromatherapy with the chakras is powerful.

Once you've identified what energy you're more in need of, choose an oil and put a few drops on your feet, or a few drops in your left palm, rub your hands together and breathe in, or diffuse them into the air through an oil diffuser.

As you read the description of each chakra, take a moment to go within and determine which centers you feel are in a good place and which ones might need some work. That way you will know which ones to focus on through the toning exercise at the end of the chapter. You will also discover which oils to use to access a more aligned and peaceful state.

I find that checking in with where I am in terms of my own blocks on a regular basis helps me function at a more optimal level. I highly recommend that you revisit this chapter anytime you feel out of alignment to identify the area in question and move the energy back into a centered space.

Now let's look at each chakra in detail.

The Root Chakra

Color: Red

Recommended Young Living Essential Oils: Palo Santo, Sacred Mountain™, Grounding™

Our connection to the earth and our stability begins with the first chakra known as "The Root", which starts at the base of the spine at the sacrum and moves down into the legs and feet.

Feeling grounded is key to manifesting in this dimension. Without a sense of groundedness and connection to the earth, the act of creation is more difficult. Feeling support beneath your feet, literally and figuratively, helps you feel physically and mentally relaxed.

This is the optimal state to be in to open the entire body, mind and spirit.

The root chakra is the center for survival and is connected to your "fight or flight" response. It is the house for your elimination organs and dictates your ability to walk and move in the world. When the root is unstable, you might feel tense, sick and fearful and have digestive issues or problems with your legs and movement.

There are studies showing that as humans, we carry the "fight or flight" response in our DNA, left over from a time when we were focused purely on survival as a species. That is why you may often have fears that are irrational. However, trauma can also induce this response and it takes time to reprogram the patterns that form as a result. Balancing the root chakra is excellent for the shadow work process!

A balanced root chakra connects you with the earth, your home, the land around where you live and your sense of safety. If you find yourself in the process of a major life change like moving, divorce, having a child, changing careers, loss of a loved one, losing a job, etc., nourishing this chakra will help clarify your focus and help you to rebalance during times of instability.

The earth element is perfect for manifesting and creating to-do lists, reorganizing, plotting your next project and embodying the practical elements of things that will help you connect more deeply to your voice and purpose.

The grounded element can help you build your business, strengthen your career or relationships and create and manifest projects.

MOVING FROM BEING UNGROUNDED TO A GROUNDED SPACE

Being ungrounded was a normal part of my life for years.

My family moved often when I was young and I developed strong wanderlust that resulted in moving a lot on my own throughout my 20s and 30s. I have also traveled to 22 countries and 42 of the U.S. states. After I moved to Los Angeles for the second time, I knew I needed to root down and stop "running" for a while in order to study and build my healing practice.

Once I slowed the travel down, I was able to start my music consulting business, which sustained me while I was taking classes and moving into my career in the healing arts, and exploring my music and sound aspirations. Grounding gave me the strength to create and grow: a place to plant the seeds and water the soil waiting for the flowers to bloom.

Once I felt securely planted with a developed practice in Los Angeles, I began to travel more again. I inherently knew that the energy and experiences I gain in other parts of the world help me in working with clients and leading events. I use my travels now to gain knowledge and experiences to further serve my purpose of helping people.

Similarly, once you've grounded yourself externally and internally, the universe will let you know when it's time to travel and explore again. Whether the travel is in your mind and growth experience or literal travel in the world, you will begin to navigate feeling grounded from anywhere, anytime.

The singing voice also needs the gravity of the body to resonate at its optimum level. This feeling of planting the feet into the earth is essential to full body alignment with the voice. When you feel grounded, the voice can function at its highest capacity.

If you have experience singing in a choir in your past, you may have heard your choir director tell you to plant your feet into the ground or to stay grounded. When you feel balanced and connected to your body in this way, your breath becomes deeper, enabling the physical mechanism of your voice to blossom.

Grounding into the earth and the soil, to create and build, is necessary to become like the flowers and bloom.

THE SINGING TOOLBOX - The Root Chakra

EXERCISE AND TREE HUGGING

Step 1. EXERCISE

Exercise is one of the best tools to realign the root chakra.

Walking, running and hiking are best for getting the root back in place. Basically, anything that gets you outside and moving will help move this energy forward. Communing with nature and putting your feet on the ground – in the sand or the dirt – also helps recharge the root.

Step 2. LITERAL TREE HUGGING

Yes, I'm serious here, I really do want you to hug a tree!

Hugging a tree with feet on the ground will offer the strength to recharge and receive from the earth. Electrons emitted from the trees are meant to recharge the body. Similarly, wearing shoes has moved humanity away from receiving grounding from the earth, so take as much time as you can to connect to the trees and dirt.

The Sacral Chakra

Color: Orange

Young Living Essential Oils: Inner Child™, Orange and Clary Sage™

Located in the area from the belly button to the top of the pubic bone, the sacral chakra houses our creativity, sexuality, feelings, intimacy, sensuality and empathy. It is the birthplace of all of your ideas, not to mention the literal place of birth, creation and reproduction. When creativity or sexuality is blocked, then this chakra gets stifled. Allowing this energy to flow freely puts you in your optimum state of creativity and connection.

I even named my business Sacral Sounds based on this chakra. Opening my sacral chakra/creativity center through music inspired me to use my healing gifts to help others access their own creativity and heal themselves. Hence the name stemmed in grounded creativity.

The sacral chakra also represents your ability to be in flow with everything in your life. Unexpressed creativity and emotions can get trapped in this area, so putting a voice to your creative inclinations will help you to open this chakra up and allow the flow in all areas of your life. Blocked symptoms include sexual dysfunction, emotional issues, or imbalance and digestive issues with the stomach. The presence of any of these ailments is an indicator that this chakra needs some loving attention.

CONNECTING THE HEALING DOTS OF A SACRAL CHAKRA DISEASE

My entire life I have suffered from Endometriosis, a condition that causes debilitating menstrual cramps and severe PMS symptoms. I tried many Western methods to help with the issue, including surgery, all ultimately proving ineffective. The only thing that worked was simply taking a lot of painkillers during my period, and those also upset my stomach, so there was always a tradeoff.

As I embarked upon more alternative methods of dealing with the pain through acupuncture, diet, Shiatsu massage and energy healing, I had more insight and the pain would subside for a short time, but it always came back. Even working with a Shaman in Peru, I had insight, but no real relief from the pain.

And I was stumped.

Until I finally made the connection.

The Endometriosis was connected to my voice and my creativity. When I was singing regularly and expressing myself healthily in all my relationships, the pain was less. When I was suppressing feelings or parts of who I was, the pain was worse. The condition may have been hereditary, however it was also a gift that was getting my attention and waking me up to the fact that I was not really listening to my own voice, or using my voice to do what it was meant to do: help and inspire others and to be of service.

The pain still varies in severity, though now I use it as a barometer for self-care, paying attention to when I need to take a timeout.

DEEP HEALING OF THE SACRAL CHAKRA WOUNDS

This chakra is also a delicate space and needs to be handled with care and compassion, along with very clear boundaries. If you have suffered from any sexual abuse, bringing this area back into balance and regaining trust with intimacy and creative flow is paramount to healing. Singing and any sounds using the voice along with movement can really help with releasing this energy and reconnecting with intimacy and creativity. Trust is necessary so that whatever needs to be released has a safe place to be let go.

Healing in this area leads to deep creative self-expression and the ability to connect with your sexuality in a safe and healthy way. Using the voice and body to express and move through sound and movement will help you grow into a healthy state of creation.

THE SINGING TOOLBOX - The Sacral Chakra

CREATIVE EXPRESSION THROUGH DANCE

Similar to the "shaking medicine" I talked about in the last chapter, you can take it even further by expressing yourself through dance.

Step 1. Make a playlist of varying types of music about 30 minutes in length. Begin with something slow and work up to something louder and more rhythmic, bringing the energy back down to something slower and more meditative at the end.

Step 2. Close your eyes and begin to dance as you play the list, paying particular attention to your hips and the area between your belly button and the top of your pelvic bone. Let your body express itself freely. Let your voice express itself freely. Notice how your body releases as you allow the dance to unfold.

Step. 3. At the end, take 3-5 minutes to meditate and notice any clarity that arises and any feelings that came up in the process. Notice if you feel more inspired to work on your creative process. Also notice if any of your sexual blocks feel clearer afterwards.

Recommendation: 5Rhythms Dance

In Los Angeles, I regularly attend a 5Rhythms Dance class where the instructor guides the class through improvisatory movements and dance interactions with others that enable you to release and express emotions through the body rather than words. This experience builds on the Somatic Experience of healing and I find that, after a week full of clients, I come home with more creative energy and freedom after a class.

You can research and see if there are 5Rhythms or Ecstatic Dance classes where you live.

The Solar Plexus Chakra

Color: Yellow

Recommended Young Living Essential Oils: Valor™, Motivation™, and Purification™

The Lion is always the first image I see when I think of the solar plexus and how to access your personal power. Located just under the ribcage at the base of your sternum, the diaphragmatic breathing I explained in an earlier chapter is the pinnacle of accessing the energy of the solar plexus. This is your power center, the place where your vital energy and fire move into action.

It is where your passion builds and is also the center for friendship.

A diminished solar plexus manifests as anxiety, depression, affected self-esteem, weight problems, little or no self-control and liver, spleen or kidney problems. Just using the diaphragmatic breathing will help with any of these symptoms. Singing will also help move these energies, along with one of my favorite power center yoga exercises, the Lion Pose, described in the toolbox.

ACCESSING YOUR POWER THROUGH THE DIAPHRAGMATIC BREATH

Even though I have been performing and public speaking for my entire life, there were times when I felt under the weather, beaten down, in grief or otherwise not in a good place. I was able to access inner strength at these moments by using the breath. The diaphragmatic breath is an amazing tool for this.

In my public and professional life, I used it often, as it was easier for me than exercising the same power in my personal life. In personal relationships, I was more passive and didn't stand up for what I needed in the moment. I had resistance to using my tools because it didn't feel safe. It took much practice and persistence to begin to access my own power and to properly communicate what I needed from those closest to me.

And it wasn't comfortable.

The more I could connect with the physical feeling of strength in my mind and body, the easier it became. I was able to do this mostly through singing and using my breath. Getting to the place of exercising tools in every area, especially those that are uncomfortable, will open your voice even more.

FINDING COURAGE IN EXPRESSION

Again we come back to the theme that courage is not absence of fear, but rather feeling the fear and putting ourselves out there anyway. *The Wizard of Oz* illustrates this perfectly with the Cowardly Lion. He was a coward until he faced the wizard and asked for courage. Ultimately he realized that what he was afraid of didn't exist and the wizard was just a small man with a big ego.

The fear is often bigger in our heads than the reality.

So we might fail in performance.

So what!?

There is not a single person in this world who has done great things that hasn't failed many times along the way.

So I encourage you to embrace the failure and ask for courage.

See the fear as a gift rather than the enemy.

I promise you will see your power grow stronger and more vibrant.

Step beyond cowardice and embody the Courageous Lion.

THE SINGING TOOLBOX – The Solar Plexus Chakra

YOGA: LION'S POSE

Step 1. Sit on your shins and then spread your knees apart, as you would do for a wide-legged child's pose, with the toes touching underneath.

Step 2. Place your palms in between your knees with the wrists forward and fingers pointed towards the wall behind you.

Step. 3 Inhale up onto your shins and, on the exhale, curve your spine slightly as if in modified cow pose.

Step 4. On the exhale look up, stick out your tongue, turn your eyes up, look cross-eyed and release the breath with sound.

Step 5. Repeat at least 3 times.

You can look at videos of this pose on YouTube for further instruction and to see what it looks like. It is incredibly effective to do this pose in addition to the diaphragmatic breathing to get connected to your personal power.

The Heart Chakra

Color: Green

Recommended Young Living Essential Oils: Joy™, Harmony™, Rose

The heart resides in the middle of the chakras, literally at the "heart" of your being. Associated with the color green, the fourth chakra is the point of reference for following your dreams, receiving and giving love and experiencing true contentment. It is guaranteed that at some point in your journey you will experience heartache. If this feeling is not addressed, it can get stuck as residue and create patterns and fears that keep you from experiencing the one thing all of us desire: the feeling of being loved.

Throughout my life I have noticed that everyone I know struggles with one life challenge more deeply than others.

For some it's money and abundance.

For some it's health.

For some it's career.

For some it's relationships.

For me, it's certainly been relationships that I've struggled with more than anything else.

As I've observed and watched myself through the heartaches, ups and downs, patterns and energy exchanges, I have come to realize that the heart is a muscle like any other. It gets trained to stay in pain when certain patterns repeat themselves and the story of pain is the one retold. The muscles can also be trained to trust and experience more joy by cultivating awareness and making different choices.

Everyone I know has the same energy around a personal struggle. And all of these patterns, no matter what they are, are deeply rooted in the heart chakra.

In fact, ANYTHING that keeps us from our desires or dreams is rooted in the heart chakra being misaligned.

From a young age, I knew I wanted to sing.

When I wasn't singing, my heart was closed.

When I was singing without feeling connected, my heart was closed.

When I sang from a place of fear, my heart was closed.

So I sang through the voices that plagued my heart muscle until it slowly opened.

Now I sing multiple times a week in public sound baths where I improvise with my voice and let whatever energy needs to be voiced come out to be shared.

Sometimes my voice comes through sounding like an Indian tribal chief.

Sometimes my voice is very high and coloratura.

Sometimes my voice is raw, vulnerable and raspy.

Each quality of voice carries a different energy that I trust helps the people who are there to receive and transform.

And sometimes I still hear the old negative voices blocking the energy as a means to protect myself.

As Rumi states in his very famous quote, "Your task is not to seek for love, but merely to seek and find all the barriers within yourself that you have built against it."

Every time I share the music of the moment in the improvised sound baths I create, my heart has an opportunity to open further.

When I feel a block coming up, I notice it and release.

Over time, I have learned that heart opening and love is really about directing the energy within the self. And from that place sending it outwards.

Heart opening can happen within all relationships and it truly starts from within. Relationships provide the groundwork for the opening.

Each time we experience a block, we can go back within, breathe into the blockage or resistance and let it open again.

LEARNING TO RECEIVE THROUGH THE HEART

My most intense heart opening came in March 2016 in the King's Chamber in the Great Pyramid in Egypt for the Spring Solstice. The group I was with had the inside of the pyramid alone for two hours and held a sound ceremony with bowls, toning and the Gayatri mantra.

This was the culmination of the 10-day trip and each step of the tour through the sacred temples brought me face-to-face with another onion layer highlighting my lifelong resistance to receiving.

It's not uncommon for people in the healing profession to forget to make time to receive since most of the work is centered on giving, and most healers are by nature, myself included, better at holding that space for others rather than giving to themselves.

In the sound meditations we created throughout the trip (in various temples) I naturally assumed my role of giving. This included a sound ceremony I did with the trip leader for everyone else.

When we entered the Great Pyramid for the last sound meditation of the trip, I again assumed my place singing with the tuning forks, and joined in alongside everyone else. But as soon as the Gayatri mantra started, I heard a loud voice tell me to lie down and receive and I stopped, laid down on the ground and started sobbing – and sobbed uncontrollably until all the singing stopped. As a puddle on the floor of the chamber, I knew I let go of the biggest block in my heart that I had likely been carrying across lifetimes. My internal voices declared that I was leaving the pain of this life there in the pyramid, to be transformed and released.

Do you feel there are areas in your life where you are not

receiving what you need?

Are there pains in your life that you are ready to transcend and let go of?

What blocks and pain are you ready to release?

Identify and sit with these blocks and pains, and use the exercise to work through the heart chakra to clear them.

THE SINGING TOOLBOX – The Heart Chakra

OPENING THE HEART THROUGH THE VOICE

Step 1. Observe your heart space by placing your left hand on your heart and your right hand over your left.

Step 2. Breathe into that space to listen to your heart, to hear what it has to say to you.

Step 3. Once you feel connected with that voice, begin to sing. Let whatever sounds want to move through you move. I recommend not using words for this process, just syllables and vowels, connecting with the energy.

Step 4. If the voices are painful, sing.

If the voices are joyful, sing.

If the voices are loving, sing.

Step 5. Continue this practice for 3-5 minutes at a time several days in a row. Notice what shifts.

This exercise will bring forth the blocks in your heart to release them and clear the heartache. It might take some practice, but I promise it will move the energy in your heart. The blocks will begin to release and the joy will be shared.

This is the place of true heart connection.

The Throat Chakra

Color: Blue

Recommended Young Living Essential Oils: Basil, Peppermint, Transformation™

For a number of years, I have been leading workshops in opening the throat chakra and it is what ultimately led to this book. This chakra is the bridge between the lower chakras and the higher chakras. The way you communicate, sing and use your voice is directly correlated with how you express all the parts of who you are.

Your voice is one of the most powerful tools of expression you have. When this chakra is open and you are singing from your heart center, magic happens. People are affected.

When this chakra is blocked, it is common to suffer from throat infections like tonsillitis and strep throat, laryngitis, headaches (due to neck tension), jaw and neck issues, TMJ, neck pain and dental problems. Addressing these ailments can be greatly helped through noting where in your life you are not speaking your truth, honoring your words and setting boundaries with people in your life.

Often people use the term "choked up" when emotion is expressed through the throat and crying (or other sounds) come forth rather than words. It's another way of the emotions expressing themselves, as all sounds made with the voice are elements of expression – from sighing to beat boxing to audible breathing to screaming to singing.

EXPRESSION OF THE VOICE, REGARDLESS OF THE INSTRUMENT

If you listen to pop, rock, country and famous singers of many genres, it's clear that not all of them have great singing voices. However, even those who don't have the best instruments often communicate emotion effectively through their singing voice and their songs – Bob Dylan is an artist that comes to mind.

The instrument is the vessel and no matter what stage your voice is in at the moment, you can connect with your own inspired voice and still move someone emotionally. The throat chakra just needs to be open.

The throat chakra is also your expression of joy through laughter and song. And singing and dancing are the embodiment of joy: you do not need them to survive, but you need joyful expression in order to thrive. Anytime you find yourself moving away from that joyful space, you can bring yourself back to a funny memory, sing a song you enjoy or practice toning.

You can use your voice to bring yourself back to joy.

THE SINGING TOOLBOX – The Throat Chakra

ECSTATIC SINGING

In the same fashion as the Ecstatic Dance, you can use your voice for this mode of expression.

Step 1. Begin to breathe audibly through the mouth, allowing the throat to open.

Step 2. Begin voicing on a soft "OH" from the bottom of your range to the top, allowing the sound to move up and down.

Step 3. Bring other vowels and sound into the mix as they arise.

Step 4. Imagine your voice is moving through any area of your body that needs to be expressed. You can add movement too if you want to.

Step 5. Really go deep into what wants to come out through your voice and let it move.

Step 6. When you feel you are complete, move back into the breath and silence.

Step 7. Sit quietly for a few minutes to integrate and be with yourself.

The Third Eye Chakra

Color: Indigo

Recommended Young Living Essential Oils: Envision™, Jasmine, Grapefruit

Located in the middle of the forehead between the eyebrows, the third eye represents your inner perception and intuition. In spiritual teachings, this is the center of enlightenment. It is the deeper sense of what you see beneath the surface, how you listen to your gut and how you react to your extrasensory perceptions. Stillness allows more connection with this energy center, and it is found most easily through meditation and sound. When this chakra is blocked, it often manifests as severe headaches and problems with eyesight, and seeing the world with tunnel vision rather than expansiveness.

NIGHTMARES AND VISIONS MANIFEST AS THE THIRD EYE OPENS

Accessing the third eye opening as a child, I often experienced nightmares where I woke up screaming in the middle of the night, often referred to as "night terrors". In one of the recurring nightmares (which, in hindsight, had many comedic elements), I am in the woods with the *Little Rascals* (Alfalfa included) and we are all being chased by wolves.

Later in life, while earning my undergraduate degree, I took a course called "Exploration of the Paranormal" (yes, this class actually existed at a private all-girls school in the south). For one of the class sessions, two shaman women from the Appalachian Mountains in North Carolina came to class and led a shamanic drum journey. For reference, a shaman is a spiritual guide and healer stemming from the traditions of indigenous cultures who works within the spiritual realm of healing.

If you have never experienced a shamanic drum journey before, the leader generally plays a frame drum with a consistent simple rhythm while you journey in your mind's eye to a place in nature from your childhood like a lake or a tree. Using that familiar place as a starting point, you continue the journey down to the underworld of inner earth. This is a grounded place where healing can happen, an inner reality that exists underneath our external human perceptions.

The guides instruct you to go down into the earth – imagine Alice in Wonderland going down the Rabbit Hole – and notice which animal visions appear. Once you see three of the same animal, you are to hug yourself. Once everyone sees their three animals, the leader brings everyone back from the meditation journey. The only sound is that of the drum.

Now, at this point in my life, I clearly had a curiosity about the paranormal and watched many psychological thrillers and shows about ghosts, but I knew very little about Native American shamanism. As I went into the drum journey, that old nightmare from childhood came back – a nightmare I hadn't had in at least ten years – and I was back seeing the wolves chase me with the *Little Rascals*. At the end, I shared what happened to me, and the shaman's response was, "Well, the wolf is clearly your spirit animal and first totem. It was simply trying to get your attention, but you are the one who kept running."

This was my first major perception shift of my own abilities within my dreams. I went from perceiving dreams as being out of my control to something that could be used for deeper understanding. I later researched the meaning of the wolf as a totem and learned that the wolf is the primary teacher, denotes a deep connection with instincts, an appetite for freedom and, when running, can demonstrate lack of trust in others and oneself. Given my life journey, this all made complete sense and was the first moment I felt connected to the third eye, even though I did not know what that actually meant at the time.

Eventually, I developed my third eye through working on my intuitive abilities. This came through meditation practice, trust and getting out of my own way to let the energy move through me. All of the previous exercises described throughout the chapters helped develop this space as I learned how to listen and allow.

ACCESSING THE THIRD EYE THROUGH SOUND

When I lead my sound baths, I listen to the energy of the space and allow the music to come through me, setting the intention that whatever comes through is for everyone's highest good. This happens from my own place of stillness and enables me to let the music flow through me and access my own intuitive center. You might come into the sound bath with your brain full of thoughts, and at the end hit a state of deep relaxation where everything goes still. It is in this state where lucid dreaming and alternative realities are experienced and where you may be gifted insight and clarity into your life purpose and current experiences, in addition to insights into your past and patterns.

One first-time participant came up to me afterwards to share privately that all of her past traumas came up for her to look at and process and asked if this was normal. Yes, this is a very normal experience since the subconscious is accessed in states of deep relaxation. The body in that state is given a chance to rest so the nervous system can heal and unprocessed information will come to the surface to be processed.

You will experience this stillness state of complete presence and awareness when the third eye is open and active. Just be warned that sometimes Third Eye activation for you may feel very intense with a pressure build-up behind the eyes and in the center of the forehead.

After I had my release and heart opening in the Great Pyramid, I left feeling a very intense pressure in my forehead, one that felt almost blinding. And I felt all of my other senses heightened, as well. Additionally, I felt connected to my inner self and the divine in a way I had never experienced before.

Since then, when I go deeply into meditation, receive or create sound baths, I reconnect with that space.

You can also reconnect with your intuition by directing the sound of your voice to the third eye and activating the space through touch, as described in the exercise at the end of this section. The bottom line is that you need to cultivate trust in yourself and your perceptions in order for this chakra to come into its full potential.

Your intuition is to be accessed and brought forth and your ability to use it is there to be activated. As you use the below exercise and begin to cultivate using and trusting your intuition, your perceptive abilities will become more acute.

THE SINGING TOOLBOX – The Third Eye Chakra

CULTIVATING TRUST AND INTUITION THROUGH SOUND
Step 1. Identify where you feel you are naturally intuitive (could be around people, business, nature, animals, etc.).

Step 2. Identify where in your life you have difficulties with trusting your intuition.

Step 3. See where these lists intersect and can work with each other.

Step 4. Set a specific intention around cultivating your intuitive abilities and opening to trusting yourself more deeply.

Step 5. Set aside the thoughts or list of your natural intuitions and difficulties and sit quietly either on the floor in a cross-legged seat or a chair.

Step 6. Bring your palms together with fingers touching, eventually bringing your thumbs to rest just in between your eyebrows.

Step 7. Gently push your thumbs into your eyebrows and begin to spread your fingers outward from that space, keeping your thumbs touching.

Step 8. Continue this accordion action with the hands for 1-5 minutes.

Step 9. Bring your hands down and sit in silence for 1 minute. Notice if you feel differently about your original intention.

Step 10. Repeat this action to continue developing your third eye and intuitive abilities. You can do this as a break from any daily activity to enhance presence and trust.

The Crown Chakra

Color: Purple or White

Recommended Young Living Essential Oils: Frankincense, Lavender, Sage

Stillness and silence meet you at the Crown chakra located at the top of your head. The crown is your connection to the divine or higher self and the source of all creation. The divine appears in many forms, so however this manifests for you is not dependent on your personal religious or existential beliefs. The crown is also the center of connection to your innate sense of trust and knowing in the universe.

This space houses your connection to your innate mysticism within. It is the place you connect to your soul and purpose and experience bliss. Consistent meditation practice can lead you to the experience of oneness as a state that can be experienced in daily life. When the crown is closed, you might experience depression, isolation and loneliness, insomnia, an inability to move forward and spiritual disconnection.

FINDING CONNECTION THROUGH MEDITATION

My own experiences with all of these crown chakra blocks have at times been intense. Living on my own for most of my life and also creating my businesses on my own has often felt very lonely and depressing. However, each time I meditated, reminded myself of the connections in my life and used the open crown as a channel for my voice, I brought myself back into balance.

You can work through these same chakra blockages by following these exercises and listening deeper to yourself and your voice.

Once you have worked through all seven chakras, balance will become a more prominent state. It is in this place of balance, with all of the chakras aligned, where giving and receiving become one.

THE SINGING TOOLBOX – The Crown Chakra

MEDITATION
Meditation is the best way to re-align the crown chakra.

Step 1. I recommend you sit quietly either on the floor, a cushion or chair and begin to focus on the breath.

Step 2. Notice the thoughts that arise and let them go. If you find your mind is very busy, imagine a movie screen in front of you and let the thoughts travel to the screen. Then imagine you are walking a few steps back from the screen, becoming aware that the thoughts are outside of yourself.

Step 3. You can continue doing this as thoughts arise and, in each moment you feel ready to, you can either turn the screen off or let the image go.

Step 4. Repeat and continue to bring yourself back to the breath.

There are many types of meditation to explore. If you are interested in learning more, you can research classes in your local area and try out a few places to find one that you like.

Finding that stillness within will help you with clarity and, over time with disciplined practice, will help you cultivate and grow peace within.

THE SINGING TOOLBOX

BALANCING THE CHAKRAS WITH THE VOICE

There are syllables that connect the voice with the chakras and open up each chakra center listed above. Chanting one of these sounds while directing the intention, that chakra can help release energy and ground you.

Starting your morning chanting from the root all the way to the crown will bring you into alignment and to the optimum state of balance as you move throughout your day. Make sure you are using your diaphragmatic breath and support.

You can use this exercise to warm up your voice and mind before any performance, before singing practice, or to simply calm your mind and being.

Step 1. Begin chanting the root chakra tone and move up to the crown. Spend at least 1 minute on each tone and eventually increase up to 5 minutes per chakra tone.

Step 2. If you need to focus on a specific chakra, take the time to do that now.

Step 3. Move quickly from the root to the crown in sequence. Do this at least 10 times, changing the pitch from low to high as you move up the body centers.

Step 4. Sit in silence for 1-5 minutes to allow integration.

RECOMMENDED PITCHES AND SYLLABLES

The chakras are often associated with the standard western scale. You can use this scale starting with C or just use a lower pitch that resonates with you.

For the root chakra, tone a "C" to the syllable "LAM" with a long 'ah' sound.

For the sacral chakra, tone a "D" to the syllable "VAM" with a long 'ah' sound.

For the solar plexus chakra, tone an "E" to the syllable "RAM" with a long 'ah' sound.

For the heart chakra, tone an "F" to the syllable "YAM" with a long 'ah' sound.

For the throat chakra, tone a "G" to the syllable "HAM" with a long 'ah' sound.

For the third eye chakra, tone an "A" to the syllable "OM", made up of three vowel sounds 'ah-oo-oh-mm'.

For the crown, tone a "B" to the same syllable as the third eye, "OM", or simply use an open "AH".

Congratulations! Your chakras are now aligned.

Chapter 7 – How to Heal with Your Voice

Tools to unlock the singer within and heal others

"The words of the tongue should have three gatekeepers: Is it true? Is it kind? Is it necessary?"
-Arab Proverb

Healing with your voice begins with your spoken words and then moves to the singing voice.

Choosing your words carefully.

Thinking before you speak.

Carrying purity of intention behind each expression.

Speaking your mind certainly doesn't mean saying everything that runs through your head out loud (as the quote above indicates). It's about purity of intention with your words. Speech and how you use it is of paramount importance for expressing your authentic truth to others.

From this place of clarity with words, you can then begin to truly sing from a heart-centered place.

TRUSTING YOUR VOICE

It has taken me more than 20 years to be where I am now – trusting and listening to my voice and what it produces in the present moment. Through improvising music with my voice while using other sound healing instruments at public sound bath events and workshops each week, I'm given the opportunity to express myself through my heart space.

So what exactly is a sound bath?

A sound bath is an event where people gather to receive sound vibrations by either sitting in a meditation pose or laying down on a yoga mat. Each participant sets up a comfortable place to receive the healing sound of vibrations and goes on a meditative journey.

Sound is physical matter so the vibrations can feel like they are touching you and moving energy in your body and mind. The purity of tones created by the crystal and metal singing bowls, gong, my voice and other instruments combine to create what I call "music in real time."

I combine my classical music background with my intuitive energy healing training to create "energetic music" that comes through in both the form of distinct songs with structure and ambient music that promotes relaxation. Often people release energy by entering a dreamlike state enhanced by the sound, and journeying through emotional blockages.

The purity of the tones creates binaural beats, also referred to as auditory illusions, when the bowls and the voice are close in pitch. These beats mimic brainwave states creating alpha, delta and theta waves in the brain, and deep healing takes place as a result.

When I improvise on the spot during my sound baths, my voice is very different from what it used to be and very connected to my soul. I work with energy from the participants in the room and spiritual energy to transmute, transform and heal.

What it took for me to be ready to sing in public in this capacity was an innate trust that what was coming out of my voice was meant to be heard in service to the divine or higher self. I cultivated my courage to move past my insecurities and sing.

This kind of devotional beauty can be expressed through your voice, as well. Once you access innate trust inside yourself, your singing will reach a new dimension of being. If you once didn't think you had access to a powerful voice, you will find that connection now.

FINDING YOUR VOICE

For six years I have co-taught an Arts Leadership and Entrepreneurship class at the University of Southern California with the acclaimed poet and former chairman of the National Endowment for the Arts, Dana Gioia. My role in the class is to work with the students to hone their public speaking skills through class exercises and presentations, and to guide them in writing their 10-year life plan.

In the individual sessions, I work with the students to help them find their true voice and come up with a passion project or non-profit organization that they then present to the class as part of their final assignment. I warn them in the first class that I will push them, but in a gentle way. Sometimes it's necessary to push as a teacher, especially when I can sense the student is not being truthful about what he or she really wants.

Today, the path of a musical artist is not so clear and the landscape for classical musicians has changed. Orchestral jobs are fewer, university jobs are highly competitive and, if you want to survive, you need to learn how to create opportunities for yourself. This is the premise of the class and, throughout the semester, the students often become emotional in sessions, finally seeing that there are alternative paths to expressing their own voice creatively. They then begin to develop more confidence in their skills and offerings to the world.

It is incredibly rewarding when students from years past contact me to share that the organization they conceived of in class is now a registered 501(c)3 non-profit and they are successfully forging their path as a working musician through accessing their entrepreneurial spirit.

This success comes from them accessing their true voice. It was through using their voice, public speaking (even when uncomfortable) and ultimately listening to their internal desires above what other people were telling them. This brought them to a place of questioning, possibility and change.

AVOIDING THE SPIRITUAL BYPASS

At the beginning of the chapter I quoted a proverb with three questions to revisit. The first two questions ask us "Is it true? Is it kind?". First you find your truth, then you decide if it's kind to communicate that truth. The last question, though, is the most important to address: "Is it necessary?"

Often the new age community will instruct you to choose joy and happiness and bliss over any negative or shadow emotion. This is valid to a point, but it disregards the human experience that also includes sadness, grief and anger.

I have studied and received certifications in Reiki and I respect the process of the work, the healing that takes place in that space and the many beautiful practitioners and teachers I have come into contact with. However, one element of the principles in the training, the teaching of "don't be angry", never sat well with me.

Does that mean I'm not supposed to be angry if my best friend betrays my trust?

Am I not supposed to be angry if someone says hurtful words, or if someone breaks a promise?

Am I not supposed to be angry when I witness injustice in the world?

My thought is no, which is contrary to this particular teaching.

It is necessary at times to healthily express things that make us angry. It is through our honest words that we are able to communicate our needs and let people know what we are feeling and thinking. If your intention is coming from a place of truth and honesty, then you are actually practicing self-love with your words, even when expressing feelings from the shadow.

The phrase "spiritual bypass" refers to the concept that you never really let yourself experience the darker emotions and that your life will be better if you never let the negative emotions surface or give them energy. There is a belief that being in that space of positivity all the time and "bypassing" the more difficult emotions will keep you in a heightened, happy state. However, in my experience, avoiding going to these places eventually will catch up to you. Experiencing the full range of human emotions as they arise is part of BEING human.

Expressing all of your emotions in a healthy and positive way will actually enable a fuller life and range of experience.

So sometimes "Yes, it IS necessary" to express these sentiments and feelings, even when it's uncomfortable.

MOVING THROUGH FEAR OF EXPRESSION

As I moved through life, I often held back my thoughts and feelings in friendships and relationships because I was fearful of losing that person.

So when I felt hurt, I kept it to myself.

However, not expressing my feelings when they came up forced them to fester like an infected blister. People subconsciously feel that energy even when it's not spoken out loud and the infection, left untreated, spreads and becomes much more serious.

At that point in any relationship when the blister bursts, things finally reach a boiling point and hurtful things are said. When feelings are expressed in this emotionally heightened way, the bond often severs completely – and it happened to me. Conversely, when difficult feelings were spoken in a timely, kind and compassionate way, over time my relationships were different and better. This came through expressing all levels of my experience.

And this will happen to you, too, as you find your words. As your voice becomes stronger and as you become more vulnerable, your relationships will change and grow. Some will go away and some will become stronger.

The friendships that echoed the mirrors of old beliefs I held about myself began to fade away. Their voices no longer echoed the truth of who I was in present time. Once I accepted who I was, it was time to let anyone who only saw me as my past self go.

On the flip side, it has made more room for the people who see me for who I am to enter that space.

Singing and sharing my heart space through music and healing work gave me the forum to allow myself to be seen on a different level – and to bring in the new echoes of voices and people. I am now more consistently in a place of connectedness within all of my experiences. I am no longer afraid of the comings and goings in my life, as I know that they are all a measure of what is unfolding inwardly and outwardly through my words and expression.

How did I learn to trust the beauty of my own voice?

By continuing to practice and recognize the voices I internalized that echoed encouragement and the reflection of beauty. One voice in particular stands out and is worth sharing with you now.

"SHAT SIRUN EH" – THE BEAUTY OF A VOICE

The first time I remember embodying a distinct positive voice in my head about my singing was when I lived in Amsterdam. I was in my early 20s and met a boyfriend who was Armenian.

I was primarily a pianist at the time but wanted to continue singing, so I sang in a Renaissance Choir while taking voice lessons. My boyfriend often told me at the concerts how much my voice stood out (not necessarily a good thing for a choir) and that it was beautiful, but that I didn't trust myself enough.

Who I was came through my voice – insecure, unsure of myself and afraid. Beautiful tones would come out, but I had no control over the instrument and my soul was stifled – I had an emotional disconnect from my voice.

After Amsterdam, I moved to Bloomington, Indiana, to be with him at the Indiana University School of Music – the largest music school in the world – and worked odd jobs while taking voice lessons. This man was also a pianist and played piano for my lessons.

In those moments when I would tap into my true voice (and they were just moments as the connection was incredibly inconsistent – similar to those flashes of bliss) he would say the phrase "Shat Sirun Eh", which in essence means "what beauty it is". Those Armenian words stuck with me and often pop into my head when I hear beauty through someone's voice.

Those beautiful words were the intention of what I aspired to with my voice. Creating beauty not just with the technical instrument using my diaphragm, but also utilizing all elements of my internal intentions and state of being.

I tell you this to illustrate that listening to the beauty of your own voice and thoughts and setting clear and positive intentions will help you uncover your amazing voice.

You are the only one who hears your innermost thoughts.

You are the only one who has the power to change them.

And when you connect to your full on emotional depth and beauty, that energy will come through your song.

EXPRESSING CHAOS THROUGH THE VOICE

When things in your life are tumultuous and you are confronted with external events that shake you up and affect you deeply, you might go internal not knowing how to speak, what to do, or what to say. Moving the energy through the voice can really help in those moments. The tools I use are simply connecting with the voice through singing songs I love, humming, improvisatory singing and the primal scream (sounds scary, I know, but I promise it helps! It is one of the exercises at the end of the chapter).

So how did I sing through my own chaotic events?

I lived in New York City during September 2001 and was supposed to have a surgery two days after 9/11 to determine whether or not I had cancer, and to have growths removed as the pre-cancer was already confirmed. I had a long talk with my oncologist who explained to me that if they found any cancer behind the stage III pre-cancer lines, I was looking at radiation treatments and early menopause.

I was 28 at the time and terrified.

The surgery was supposed to be on September 13th, 2001.

Then the whole world bottomed out when the Twin Towers came down, and my father who was supposed to go to the surgery with me was stranded since all the airports were closed. The procedure was postponed.

The micro-level and macro-level of my experience was intense and frightening and I spent most of that week in my Washington Heights apartment alone watching the news.

Transportation wasn't going downtown.

My office was closed.

My friends were all downtown and we were landlocked.

And clearly there were people in much more dire need than myself at that moment.

How did I move through the intensity of my feelings at the time?

Through expressing myself through my voice. Music and my piano gave me solace. Connecting with my voice and singing brought a modicum of inner peace.

When things get chaotic, your voice can shut down. It's important to take time and make the effort to express with your voice, especially when things are the most difficult.

This is how you can move through the energy within yourself efficiently and effectively.

IF YOU CAN'T SING, TRY HUMMING

If you feel stuck with actually singing while experiencing or witnessing chaos, another tool is vocal humming. Anyone can hum, regardless of the quality of the voice. I personally believe that humming for humans also has a healing capacity for quieting the brain and calming the nervous system. In times when our inner and outer worlds are going through turmoil, just a simple humming that creates vibration in the front of the face and lips helps pull us back into our body and give us a sense of calm.

An example of a type of humming in the animal kingdom that has been studied comes from the sounds of a cat. A cat's purr is said to resonate most frequently between 25-50 hertz (and can go up to 140 hertz). Hertz is the measurement of sound vibration that determines the pitch. This range of hertz frequency is said to be that of bone growth and regeneration and has been scientifically proven to increase bone density. This is why it feels so good when a cat purrs while on your lap.

IMPROVISATORY SINGING

Another way through the chaos and trauma is with improvisatory singing.

In graduate school at Indiana University, my roommate was a

hilarious tenor from Minnesota. We often joked about the fact that we were both originally "trailer trash" since both of our parents lived in trailers at the time we were born in small Midwestern towns. Our favorite activity was to sing to each other in operatic tones instead of speaking. There was something very cathartic about this type of singing and it always made us laugh.

This operatic way of communicating was fun and connected in a way that expressed who I was as a person through singing and sharing joy. I referred to my almost constant singing about life as my "inner songbook": a way to express how I felt at any given moment. I often sing names upon greeting my close friends and make up little songs throughout the day to bring lightness into the spaces I visit.

Even if the songs are sad, they still give me an outlet to express myself and process whatever is coming up in my life.

This is a practice you too can develop, *even if you only sing in the shower!*

I hope at this point you are more aware of the innate healing capacity that lies within you and your voice. Through using the tools I have laid out for you and singing whenever you can, you will discover that you have more power than you previously realized.

Whenever you have a moment, take time to come back and use the exercises outlined in this chapter. Trust your voice, move through fear of expression, embrace your vocal beauty, sing through chaos and life events and joyfully express your improvised singing nature. Through this practice, you will begin to create more joy in expressing yourself through your voice.

As you begin expressing yourself more deeply, may you fall in love with who you are, know that your voice is meant to be heard and feel with every ounce of your being that you are meant to be singing.

THE SINGING TOOLBOX

THE PRIMAL SCREAM

If you find yourself in a place of stagnation with your voice, and especially when you feel your communication is stifled, one of the best ways to move through frustration, anger and pent-up energy is to use the Primal Scream.

For almost two years, I worked twice a week at a rehabilitation clinic for teenagers in Malibu where the youths were suffering from various ailments, including drug and alcohol addiction, trauma and mental illness.

There, I would use the Primal Scream as a tool to break up energy and help the youths open their voices.

On evenings when they were coming in from intense group shares with a lot of chaotic energy, I would have them grab pillows and scream. Oftentimes they would erupt into fits of laughter. The space lightened. They were then in a place to receive.

Step 1. Grab a towel, unless you have access to an open space where you won't scare people off.

Step 2. Scream as loud and forcefully as you can into the towel until you feel there is nothing left. I generally recommend doing this at least three times. If you feel stuck and quiet in the beginning, I recommend going up to 10 times to really access the deeper places. The energy can then move through the entire body, diffusing anything that is stuck, and other energy will often move in to take its place.

Step 3. Notice if your energy has shifted and changed.

Step 4. This might feel uncomfortable and scary and this is okay! If you have these feelings arise then it is probably an indicator of something you need to do more often. This will help those more uncomfortable feelings move through continued practice.

This tool is important in letting energy in the body and mind come out as a purge of emotion in a healthy way. It is also a healthy way to release any pent up anger and rage. You can always repeat the exercise as much as necessary to get the energy to move and transform into another space.

SINGING YOUR FEELINGS AND THE INNER SONGBOOK

Singing your feelings can be a daily practice and way of connecting with emotions that are not ready to be spoken.

Step 1. Express through your voice whatever you are feeling. No words, only tones and sounds and breath. This exercise can be cathartic and healing.

Step 2. Practice this as a daily ritual when greeting family or friends. It might feel ridiculous at first, but will ultimately make people laugh. Through singing your feelings purely and simply, you allow yourself to be joyful.

Step 3. With the same energy begin to add words to your experience, expressing yourself through simple vocal action. To start, try simply singing instead of speaking your words.

Step 4. Find a friend to practice with and allow the songs to flow.

Chapter 8 – Integration of the Soul Path

Bring your inner truth to the surface to share and inspire

"Integrate what you believe in every single area of your life.
Take your heart to work and ask the most and best of
everybody else, too."
-Meryl Streep

Now it's time to put the pieces of the puzzle together.

Throughout the previous chapters you have uncovered some of the incongruent places within yourself, and the places where you might need to look deeper. Places where you need to speak up and where you need to stay silent. And places where you need to give yourself more love, as well as places where you already feel full.

And you now have tools to apply as the proverbial onion of personal growth and spirituality unravels further.

Each piece of skin becomes more and more clear as you identify, process and use your tools to transform into something strong, vibrant and permeable. As an onion becomes more transparent through cooking, so will you.

And this process of shedding parts of yourself that are no longer connected to your soul's purpose is natural, healthy and, frankly, scary as hell!

It is a process that will be challenging at times, and amazing at other times.

It's also necessary for learning and growing. Taking your life lessons and transforming them into your way of being in the world will help you be of service in whatever your life path promises to

115

be.

It is how you begin to use your voice in a way that is mindful and compassionate and brings you and others more joy.

The steps of integration are based on some of what we have already learned and take you another step deeper as we move through this chapter. You will bring the puzzle pieces into form, one by one, so that you can make friends with yourself and every part of who you are.

IDENTIFYING THE INCONGRUENT PUZZLE PIECES

How do you bring all of these life lessons together?

First by understanding how you keep parts of your life segregated and identifying the pieces that no longer fit, letting them go and bringing in the pieces that do fit to add them in.

Then learning to bring them all together.

Once you understand the layers of who you are, your path will begin to make more sense and you will experience moments of completion equated with pinnacle life moments like graduating from high school or college. In the words of Ohso, "In these moments we are able to perceive the whole picture, the composite of all the small pieces that have occupied our attention for so long. In the finishing, we can either be in despair because we don't want the situation to come to an end, or we can be grateful and accepting of the fact that life is full of endings and new beginnings."

It's time to revisit another layer of what I shared in earlier chapters about my own incongruent pieces of the puzzle.

When I moved to Los Angeles in 2007, I kept my spiritual interests quiet. I felt that it was important to keep a corporate face while working at the Los Angeles Philharmonic. I figured that if anyone knew my true beliefs I would be taken less seriously. So I silenced that part of myself.

116

The timing of taking that job coincided with my father's passing and took me into a deep depression, as I shared before. I did my best to keep that hidden too.

As I continued in what I thought was my dream job, I fell deeper and deeper into unhappiness. Confusion set in and I questioned everything that brought me to that place.

It took two and a half years before it all broke down and my official journey of healing and wellness began.

Admitting I was unhappy also meant changing my life.

And I was PETRIFIED!

It was much easier to ignore these parts of myself than to deal with the truth.

The moment I began to admit the truth to my boss and people around me, everything broke down. The constructs of my life fell apart and I couldn't yet see the forest through the trees. My puzzle pieces were in shambles.

In hindsight, if I had known that I was actually listening to my true voice and building a more expansive puzzle, I would have trusted the process more. Or maybe I wouldn't have. Looking back, I can't change what happened, however I did learn from it and developed differently from that point forward. I began to be more open about my true interests and my calling and I embarked on a different path. I became the transformer by transcending fear.

My tools come from that breakdown.

My breakdown was a necessary part of the breakthrough!

If you find yourself in pieces due to life events, see if you can welcome the circumstances as something that have a bigger destiny in store for you.

EVEN IF YOU CAN'T SEE IT YET!

Let yourself be in the breakdown, feel the breakdown with every element of your being. The welcoming may take a long time, but you will get there.

However you feel in the process is valid and OK!

In putting together your integrated puzzle, there are a few important questions to ask yourself:

Have you experienced any breakdown to breakthrough moments in your life and, if so, what did they teach you?

Are there parts of you that maybe once brought you joy, but no longer do?

Are you ready to let go of who you were to become who you are?

REVISITING YOUR INTENTIONS AND CULTIVATING AWARENESS

Going back to the earlier exercise about identifying the intention behind each part of what you do is the next step. Each piece of the puzzle carries an intention with it. Getting clear on the intention behind each part of your life will help you with making the necessary shifts.

Remember how I switched my career intentions away from running a major arts institution to building a career in the healing arts? I wanted to help people and be of service and the puzzle pieces where I was no longer fit who I was becoming. I changed my intention and then had to do the same thing with music.

In revisiting my own music-making process when I left full-time employment, I realized that, in a deeper layer of the onion, my incongruent puzzle piece was based in the shadow instead of the light. I realized that my relationship to music was connected to an intention that was based in my wounding rather than my joy.

My intention behind music-making at the time was "escaping from pain" and it took me a few years to reconnect with my original music-making intention of "coming from joy".

Music was my "drug" to escape rather than a creative outlet, and changing that relationship was a process.

Ironically, the thing that once qualified as my "drug" and escape became the medicine with which I now heal myself and other people. My original medicine and true love from childhood came back to the forefront.

If you take the time to identify the deeply imbedded intentions behind the things you do, you can change them. You can create deeper intentions to align with what you are trying to create in present time.

This practice is powerful, but it takes time.

HOW DID I CHANGE THIS INTENTION AND HOW CAN YOU CHANGE YOURS?

I did this by taking a full year to start improvising again on the piano, which resulted in the creation of a few songs. As I allowed whatever moved through me to come to me naturally and in its own time without forcing the process, I became more at ease with trusting the unfolding process. In moments of frustration, or if I no longer felt joy, I walked away. Then I would come back when I was in a fresher place, ready to create again.

I went through the same process improvising with my voice until it felt like second nature and I trusted that my voice would know what to do.

This process was a lesson in learning to trust the present moment and be with whatever feeling or sensation was arising in my system.

Now I can find the joy in my music-making, even on the bad days.

I listen to the expression and let the voices within be heard.

And then I externalize them through song.

This is the best way to let the creative process unfold. Try, try again and then try some more. Let the mixed emotions arise and be expressed, and let the true parts of who you are underneath come through your voice and shine. Those voices are meant to be shared.

IDENTIFYING BLOCKS TO BREAKTHROUGH

A recent client with past experience as a professional singer was also a talented painter and writer. Because of her cultural limitations and many past traumas, she felt disconnected from her artistic expression for some time and wanted to find a way to push through and access that part of herself again.

After six sessions of identifying and working through all of her blocks, she was ready for me to push her into that space again. Simply using a singing bowl and her voice, I guided her through words to a space where she could access that part of herself without inhibitions, and her magnificent voice came shining through in all its glory. Her entire being let go and she had a massive crying release while feeling connected to the deepest parts of her voice in a way she never had.

Her intention to go deep was heard, the space was created for her to access it, healing moved through her and now continues to evolve beyond our sessions.

In identifying your own deeper places in the onion, ask yourself these questions:

What are your deepest intentions in work, hobbies or relationships?

What activity allows you to be yourself and explore your creativity with abandon, allowing yourself the freedom to simply create?

What do you feel is the most important thing to be expressed through your voice?

GETTING TO THE CORE THROUGH STORYTELLING

In revisiting the story-telling pieces of previous chapters, it becomes clear that looking at stories that define your core-being are essential to the process of honing your full, creative voice.

Think back to a few pinnacle times throughout your life where you can identify feeling vital, happy, free and excited about sharing your voice. It could be singing a solo in a concert, a play you put on for your family, a story you wrote, or a time when you stepped up to the plate and made a major difference in one person's life. This will help you with seeing the trajectory of your life and moments that sharing your voice was relevant to who you are.

One of my own stories foreshadows many elements that exist in my life at present:

Greensboro, NC, though a nice southern city to grow up in, had very segregated neighborhoods and pockets. My family lived in a nice new development area made up of mostly white, upper-middle-class families, with a few notable exceptions.

The weekend before my 16th birthday, my parents allowed me to invite my out-of-town friends to stay for the weekend. The first night we all went on a walk through my neighborhood and saw a house at the end of our street with Christmas lights.

This was early November.

I had the bright idea to ring the doorbell and sing Christmas carols.

So we went up to the door, rang the doorbell and began singing "Joy to the World". It turns out the family living there was Indian and the many people in the house were decked out in saris and turbans.

They were celebrating Guru Nanak's birthday, an Indian holiday. That's why they had lights.

The neighbors loved us singing so much that they invited us

121

inside. We sang for the entire party of people. They took pictures and then offered us food from their large Indian feast.

It was the first time I'd ever had Indian food. And now I eat it all the time.

This experience foreshadowed elements of my path, which currently involves integrating different cultures and beliefs into a place of acceptance and understanding. My path involves teaching and working with elements of healing modalities that come from multiple cultures and places, including the chakras, which originated from India. My personal life and outward life are inclusive of participants and clients from all over the world. And it all came from being open enough to share my voice and listen to what it wanted to express.

All voices are meant to be heard.

All voices are valid.

All voices can carry truth.

In identifying your own stories, the questions you can ask yourself are:

What are three stories at different points in your life where you felt most vibrant, happy and like yourself?

How do these stories foreshadow parts of your life today?

Is there something within these stories you can integrate more into your present life?

ACCEPTANCE OF THE PAST AND WHO YOU ARE

Accepting and honoring my past wasn't easy. Owning my own mistakes was a hard lesson to learn, especially in romantic relationships.

I had a long distance boyfriend over a decade ago who was kind and generous. Because he treated me well after a long series of dating mishaps, I ignored that I didn't feel the same way about him as he did about me, and let myself move forward in the relationship. I thought that maybe I could grow to love him over time.

I let him take me to Barcelona for Christmas, and Paris and Rome for our summer vacation. I received his offerings and wasn't very nice to him during our time together. I treated him like a throw-off lover and broke up with him right after our vacation.

Needless to say, I was a jerk.

When I came to London for a business trip and asked to meet him for coffee to make amends, he made other plans to be away and I didn't understand why. I honestly didn't see why we couldn't just be friends.

I was so disconnected from how I treated him that I didn't realize that I was being an asshole and needed to apologize.

A few years later I had an experience where I tapped into his pain and how hurt he was, and the reality of how I had treated him.

I wrote him a long apology.

He responded this time and accepted the apology gracefully.

I had to forgive myself for who I'd been when interacting with him.

Deep down I felt guilty that I didn't feel the same way and, instead of facing it and ending the relationship, I accepted all of the goodness he gave me without returning the sentiment. I epitomized selfishness.

The transformation was through understanding why I behaved that way, and taking responsibility for it. Then and only then was I able to grow and learn.

Everyone makes mistakes of varying degrees. Honoring them and forgiving yourself is part of the growth process. And absolutely necessary!

The key to finally feeling in the flow and on the path is to fully accept who you are.

Every single part of who you are, especially the parts that you don't like.

Accept them all.

A deep, *radical* acceptance of the journey that brought you here, with all of the ups and downs and sideways turns, that is what will lead you to a state of creative flow and abundance in every area of life.

You don't have to like your past and what got you here, but you do need to accept it and accept where you are now. The only place to start is here.

Now.

Changes can only be made from this day forward.

And they can only be made by accepting who you are unconditionally and honoring everything that brought you to this moment in time.

Everything that has happened to you in your life contributes to the uniqueness of your voice.

The positive and negative experiences.

Your life lessons.

Your past wounds and traumas.

Your studies and job experiences.

Relationships.

All of this drives you closer to what you are meant to do with your voice.

That is what integration is.

It brings all of the parts of you into a space of acceptance.

From this place your voice can be unleashed to the world.

To move forward with acceptance, ask yourself these questions:

Are there any relationships in my life where I need to make amends?

Are there actions in my past that I need to forgive myself for?

What changes in myself can I work with as I embark on this next stage of my journey?

COMPASSION FOR THE INNER SELF

As you begin to unravel before the integration is complete, your relationships will go through many changes. When you change, the world around you will change. It is impossible for this not to happen, so it is of the utmost importance that you hold a high level of compassion for yourself throughout this process.

There will be grieving for your old self and relationships that will go off in other directions or transform. Relationships that reflect who you were and not who you are becoming will be an ongoing mirror of change, and at times it will be painful.

If you begin to see all of life's experience as a learning opportunity, none of these relationships or traumas are lost – they are all pieces of the puzzle. Every element of your life experience will become a part of who you are now, and you will be able to help hold that space as others around you go through a similar process.

If I hadn't gone through these changes and shifts in my own life, how could I possibly hold space for others going through these changes now? If I hadn't taken the corporate music job that moved me to Los Angeles in the first place, would I have had the chance to create my life as it exists now?

The way I see it, there are no accidents.

As you shift through your lessons you will become more able to accept and honor your strengths and weaknesses.

It is how you grow.

Once you accept your past and who you are now, the joy in sharing your voice will come to the forefront of your life's journey.

Ask yourself these questions:

Are you being hard on yourself about anything in your life at present?

What current relationships in your life reflect more of who you were in the past rather than who you are now?

What can you do to be compassionate towards yourself and to bring more of your true self into your relationships?

CREATING MORE FUN

Now we get to the lighter side of things, the "flower pieces" in the puzzle, because sharing your voice is also meant to be FUN. It's time to infuse this process with some lightness and joy.

When identifying the joyful and lighthearted parts of yourself, every single element of what you bring to the table is important, even the small pieces. I always think of a beautiful story about my maternal grandparents. My grandfather loved putting together large complicated puzzles with nature landscape themes. He would often spend hours working on them, enjoying the process as all of the pieces came together.

Once he got close to the end, he would always leave the last two pieces for my grandmother. He wanted her to put the finishing touches on every puzzle.

It was an act of love.

Her seemingly small contribution was the most important one for him, and no less significant than the hours he'd put into the creation himself.

Creating this type of fun, loving ritual can heighten your experience with any activity you love. As my grandfather's process made puzzles more fun for both of them, look at activities in your life where you can share the process in a way that brings even more joy to you and someone else.

Each act you share with another from a loving space is a piece of your puzzle that you are creating.

Fun in the creative process is the key to contentment. Not just in the process of music, but in the process of everything. If you are enjoying every day in the act of doing and creation rather than simply waiting for the perceived "end result", then you will have achieved true happiness.

At moments when I find I am in drudgery around paperwork, bookkeeping or another activity that I am not looking forward to, I take a break to sing, play the piano or meditate. While meditating, I imagine what I will feel like after that particular task is done and it generally feels like freedom. That helps me focus when I return and completion comes quicker.

I had to learn this because I often forgot to incorporate fun and play as I went about achieving my goals.

As a classical musician, I was taught to practice hours and hours to learn a piece and to improve my ability. When I was younger it was fun for me to sit for hours playing the same piece over and over.

My family, however, did not think this was fun.

Regardless, I enjoyed the process of it.

Over time, as I started living my life from the negative voices of other people telling me what to do, I no longer enjoyed the process. The fear of making mistakes and not being good enough took over.

Though as I changed my music-making intention, I also changed my process around practice and craft for anything I do. My clear intention is to make the process of everything include an element of fun. My puzzle contains many more flowers now.

I know you are ready to have more fun, so ask yourself these questions:

Where can you add more fun to the process of your daily life?

What activity can add more fun and love in your relationships?

What fun activity can you add to your daily practice (dancing to a favorite song, singing out loud in the shower, talking to a dear friend)?

SELF-VALIDATION

Like it or not, you have officially embarked upon a path of personal growth and spirituality now. I know this is not an easy undertaking and I want to congratulate you on getting this far!

You have demonstrated that you have courage, stamina, discipline, questioning, curiosity and a willingness to look at your faults and weaknesses. You have participated in the process of confronting your inner demons, upleveling your relationships and communicating clearly. And I imagine your voice is already different now.

This journey of the soul comes with ups and downs, transformations, roadblocks, changes, unexpected events, grief, miracles, gifts and magic. It is the nature of the human condition and what we are here to experience.

This process of opening your voice is key to manifesting your life's purpose and passion. It is what enables you to communicate and grow, and to become the best version of yourself.

And the journey continues as long as you are here.

At the forks in the road, there will be a pause.

A moment to stop and smell the roses.

Take time to be still and validate yourself.

Witness your willingness to grow and learn.

See yourself for the wonderful creature that you are. Look in the mirror and really see yourself and all the beauty you came here to create.

This is true integration and the vision of a completed puzzle picture.

Pat yourself on the back. Really. I mean it. Do it now. You deserve it.

Integration found me by exposing my weaknesses and all the places where I wasn't tuning into my real inner voice, and then bringing together all of the things that I learned and experienced along the way to transformation. And though I did illicit the help of many healers and friends, I did most of this process without any direct guidance.

It took me nine years to figure all this out, and my path continues to unfold.

I eventually realized that if I could somehow bring all of these tools together and hold the space for people to process more quickly what it took me months and years to understand, I would finally be fully integrated.

If I could use the tools I developed along the way to help other people open their voice in the way I opened mine, I would feel integrated.

I know this is who I am meant to be in the world now.

I came out of the closet about my spiritual inclinations.

Shunned my fear about sharing my gifts.

Connected with my deeper being through sound and helping others.

Through this, I found my life's purpose.

My voice now defines my path.

Thank you for being a part of my integration.

Integration will find you too through building your congruent puzzle, revisiting intentions, working through your blocks, cultivating your story, radical acceptance, deep compassion for self, creating more fun and validating yourself. Don't forget to pat yourself on the back!

The journey of exploration is just beginning and you're now embarking on a time when speaking your truth and expressing your soul through your voice is more important than ever.

The pieces of the puzzle will come together, I promise. With continued practice and patience, integration will be yours.

Let's do this!

THE SINGING TOOLBOX

ACCEPTANCE MEDITATION

Acceptance and acknowledgement are cultivated daily practices that bring us into alignment.

Step 1. Go back through this chapter and answer all of the posed questions.

Step 2. Take a moment to look at the parts of yourself that you still need to accept and have compassion for.

Step 3. As you sit down to meditate each day (for at least a week), look at this list and then close your eyes and imagine sending loving energy to all of those pieces.

The more you cultivate this practice, the easier it will be to accept through love and compassion, learn, transform and move through your own voice cultivation and creation process.

LEARNING TO LISTEN THROUGH SILENCE

Step 1. The best way to cultivate this practice is taking a 24-hour period in silence, if your life permits. If not, even 30 minutes or whatever you can spare will work.

Step 2. Rather than talking and using your voice, you can write notes to the outside world or with people in your life.

Step 3. Take some time to also sit in silence without interacting with anyone. Really pay attention to the world around you and people's reactions to things from the role of the observer.

Step 4. Also pay attention to your own thoughts and feelings while you watch yourself interact and observe without speaking out loud.

Step 5. Journal about anything you observed in this process.

Through this practice, I learned how to observe more carefully, and I also became intimate with my deep need to feel heard. When I got silent and listened to myself this way, I realized that I could satisfy that need on my own. As a result, my ability to listen to others improved and grew.

Chapter 9 – Transformation into the Butterfly

"When she transformed into a butterfly, the caterpillars spoke not of her beauty, but of her weirdness. They wanted her to change back into what she always had been. But she had wings."
-Dean Jackson

One of my favorite books growing up was *Hope for the Flowers* by Trina Paulus, written in 1972, the year I was born. The book encapsulates the journey of two caterpillars, Stripe and Yellow, on a spiritual quest for life.

In search of the sky and something greater, the caterpillars leave the tree and climb to reach the sky, stepping and climbing over others on their way up, but once they get there, they realize they are still not at the sky. Yellow follows her instincts and prepares to spin her cocoon to emerge as a butterfly. After some enticement, Stripe eventually follows suit and goes through his own transformation.

Butterflies are powerful symbols of the transformation process since they are the only creatures that completely change their DNA structure through metamorphosis.

As a human, your metamorphosis can be no less drastic through changing your voice and your internal neuro-patterns.

Each stage of my own transformation carried a major message and healing for my internal struggles as my neuro-patterns changed. My own thoughts became different and kinder, I became less reactive and I could watch and observe my thoughts and reactions without immediately responding from an emotionally wounded place.

As my own voice opened and I changed my response to external stimuli, the transformation process happened more rapidly. And you can expect the same to happen to you.

My voice changed because I changed. And I changed because my voice changed.

It all worked in tandem.

TRANSFORMING TRAUMA INTO FORGIVENESS WITH HELP

A few months after moving to New York in 2000, I met a man who I was convinced was the person I was meant to be with. We met at a bar through one of my colleagues and spent that first night talking until the wee hours of the morning.

This man had two cats with elaborate Italian names. The cats were generally sweet and affectionate, however one of the cats would have fits late at night and started pooping in the sink. I had been told that cats could get very jealous, though this was the first time I was seeing it with my own eyes.

The night of my birthday in November when I got up to use the bathroom in the middle of the night, the one cat started making really disturbing noises and then proceeded to attack my leg. The cat turned into the rabid bunny rabbit from *Monty Python and the Holy Grail.*

Blood everywhere, literally, and I had to go into the shower to wash it all off. I made the guy clean the blood off the floor and the wall. That day my ankle started swelling and I had to go to the doctor in order to get antibiotics for cat scratch fever.

This guy loved his cat, so I said I would give the cat another chance.

Fast-forward to New Year's Eve morning, the same cat came in for the attack, basically tearing at my leg. I kicked the cat off but she came back in full force to the other leg and bit deeply into my Achilles tendon before the guy could tear her off of me.

Even more blood, even more anger.

My ankles swelled up so drastically that it created a limp and internal pain that rendered me disabled: a difficult position to be in while living in New York.

We finally broke up.

Yes, I recognize that the story around this event is somewhat comedic, however, at the time it was hugely traumatic both physically and emotionally. And the bigger point in sharing is that I was unaware of how much the physical effects still lived in my body a decade later.

The transformation around this event happened in my first Polarity Therapy class in massage school, taught by my now friend and mentor Tracy Griffiths. I offered to be the demo for the class session. As she started working on me, my left leg started shaking uncontrollably and it was completely involuntary. This was my first experience with this form of energy healing and the first time I experienced an uncontrollable shaking body part on the table.

As she asked questions while the leg continued shaking and the feelings I had around the cat attack came back to me in full force, I started sobbing. Often in healing and sound sessions it is about making the direct mind body connection for the release to occur and this was an intense one.

She asked if there was anything I still needed to do to fully let go of the trauma and the words "I need to forgive the cat" blurted out of my mouth.

It was the first time I realized clearly how much I held in my body, how my trauma lived in my body until that day, and that I needed help moving deeper into my healing process.

Powerful stuff. Traumas can define you until you transform them into healing opportunities and lessons. And sometimes you might not understand why your voice is stuck, so addressing any type of physical or emotional trauma in the body can help release anything holding you back from a physical standpoint.

In this case, I learned a deeper level of forgiveness and how, when I voiced what needed to be heard out loud, the symptoms in my leg improved. As I identified what I was holding onto and told the story that I had let define me, I was ready to take the necessary steps to clear the energy, and my life changed.

This transformation happens often in healing sessions and is the reason why finding the right person to hold space for you is so important. Sometimes in that space, it is easier to find your voice as someone is able to bear witness to your process and act as your mirror.

TRANSFORMATION OF A NAME AND THE BUTTERFLY

The transformation into my current business services started with the butterfly. Mariposa ("butterfly" in Spanish) Healing Arts was the name of my first bodywork business and the first public offering of my major career and life change.

Unfortunately, I don't speak Spanish, though I chose the Spanish name for butterfly as inspiration from when I was in the jungle in Peru doing medicine work. One of the workers at the center saw a group of butterflies circling me and shouted out the word "Mariposa" and I loved how it sounded.

As I released my first healing website to the world, I was still not quite ready to show everyone who I was, even though I knew it was what needed to happen. Those insecure voices I spoke about in the mirror section of this book came out in full force the day I launched because I was afraid of what people in the classical industry might think of this change in me.

I didn't yet own it and I was still scared of letting go of my other career.

Even though the transformation was happening, I wasn't internally feeling it and in retrospect I think my choice of name was aspirational of what I was calling in, rather than where I was. I felt like I was still spinning the cocoon. My own internal growth was still unfolding and my practice was not ready to take off yet.

It took me another two years before I ended up at the Globe Institute to do my sound healing certification, and another four months after that to launch Sacral Sounds, the name of my company based in my healing music offerings.

Sacral Sounds is a business I feel proud of and resonant with, embodying a name that feels connected to who I am and a reflection of my present and future aspirations. It took the evolution of my personal and professional development to get to this place.

The butterfly still carried with me, but the musical and more creative part of my soul finally came to the forefront with Sacral Sounds.

When I fully embodied my gifts, the resonant, grounded name appeared.

And I embraced it.

Do you have a gift buried in your psyche that you are still afraid to embrace?

Can you imagine what it would be like to cultivate this gift and bring it to the surface to share with others?

What would your vision for sharing your gift(s) be?

HOW DID I FINALLY GET CLARITY?

The inkling to bring music into the healing world was always present for me and my voice solidified this. I went from a very corporate music job to freelancing, creating a consulting business, building a bodywork practice to building a sound healing practice. The led to creating events, leading workshops and ultimately creating this book and the course that goes along with it to help others transform themselves.

In the process of integrating every part of who I am, I transformed my life and launched a program to help others transform theirs.

To give you the context of the timing – or "divine timing" as I like to call it – the day my father passed away was September 25, 2007. Nine years later – to the exact day – I presented the first incarnation of the course that inspired this book, called *Unlock Your Inner Voice*, at the Globe Sound Healing conference in the Bay area. The room was packed full of participants and, for the first time since my father passed, I felt grounded and connected with the work I am meant to do in this world. My puzzle came together and I fully emerged as the butterfly.

As the significance sunk in, I remembered that numerology works in nine-year cycles. It had been exactly nine years since my father's death started me on a path of self-discovery. It took that time to develop the tools and lessons to help others transform.

On that day, I birthed an integrated life to move me into the next chapter of experiences and sharing my gifts. I experienced the death of my old self and the emergence of the new.

The transformer in me emerged.

How did I ultimately get there?

To answer requires going backwards to before I made the decision to pursue sound healing wholeheartedly. I was taking an advanced Polarity Therapy class focused on business and cleansing and was given a simple exercise assignment that helped me get clear. This simple practice helped me define who I am at the core and how to develop my new business name and image.

The exercise was simply to narrow down three words that I felt most connected to.

Mine were and still are:

Resonance.

Music.

Love.

It was actually that simple.

I finally realized that above all of the other identities that I'd taken on – arts administrator, concert programmer, concert producer, consultant, teacher, pianist, singer, healer, bodyworker, yogi, writer – I was, first and foremost, a musician. So the next logical step was to pursue sound healing and finally bring my love of music and healing into the forefront.

Resonance was connected to everything I was doing and became a barometer for gauging my choices. Music was connected to the core of my being. Love was connected to my deepest intention of what I want to bring to the world.

This is something you can do now to access your own deeper clarity.

Trying this exercise of choosing your words will help you identify your purpose. I share the steps to help you at the end of the chapter.

TRUST IN THE UNKNOWN

I often liken each stage of transformation to jumping off a cliff. The analogy seems quite appropriate when the fear starts to take over. Yellow didn't know she was going to thrive as a butterfly, but she trusted her instincts and inner voice and did it anyways.

Each time I prepare to make the next leap into the unknown, I find myself facing my deepest fears yet again; the anxiety dreams creep in, sometimes with full blown panic attacks that wake me up the same way the wolves did in childhood, and I have to spend some time releasing and pulling myself together.

The first time I did it was when I left my music administration job in St Paul.

To revisit one last time the flip side of the story I shared about getting fired: I knew that I was in the wrong job and needed to quit, but I was too afraid. I truly believe that I was fired because the divine was pushing me to move on to the next phase of my life.

At that time, a very prominent mentor in my life was working as a consultant for the orchestra. He was also the Provost and Dean of The Juilliard School and former Artistic Advisor at Carnegie Hall. After the news that I was leaving broke, he took me on a long walk along the Mississippi River in downtown St. Paul. He listened quietly to my anxiety and fears and, in very supportive fashion, gave me some really good advice.

His words still resonate with me:

"Sometimes you can't know what's behind the next door until the one you're looking at closes."

Though he didn't make up the statement, he did continue by saying that he knew I would be fine and that I really did need to move on in order to follow what I was meant to be doing.

He also told me that my relationships and friendships would change once I left that position, but that our friendship was intact, despite the job change.

He still remains a mentor and friend and, after I produced my first sound healing CD, he reminded me of our walk in St. Paul, my fears and how I had completely transformed my life since then.

Talk about a positive mirror reflection!

EMBRACING CHANGE

Since that river walk, every small change that I've undergone, from parting ways with a project or a major client in my consulting business to each stage of development in my healing practice, I went through a similar cycle of fear and anxiety. Each piece of the puzzle changed form and evolved.

Writing this book put me through this cycle.

My first blogpost put me through this cycle.

My new website launch put me through this cycle.

Each layer of the onion, each stage of vulnerability – going into the cocoon is something that came up many times – the emergence of the butterfly transformed into something different each time.

My personal life went through the same process.

Many of the people that I had close relationships in the classical music industry fell away and other relationships in the spiritual and personal growth community took their place.

When one door closes, others open.

As you go through a transformation process, you will experience major changes in relationships.

There will be loss but there will also be gains, and most of the time the gains are BIG ONES.

As you become more of who you are, and your exterior shell and armor drop away, your new relationships will begin to reflect these changes in you. And some of your current relationships will thrive through the growth period, become stronger and serve as grounding forces in your life.

Those relationships that grow as a result of deep changes will anchor your progress and deepen in ways you never thought were possible.

Embrace the phases of the cocoon and the butterfly as they unfold, learn how to transform trauma into forgiveness, cultivate even deeper trust in yourself and the universe and embrace the changes in you as you grow.

The one thing I can guarantee is that, as you change, the world will indeed change around you.

So be prepared and be open.

Use your voice, speak your truth, live your purpose and sing!

THE SINGING TOOLBOX

PICK YOUR THREE WORDS

Step 1. For this exercise, it's best to start with at least 20 words that you resonate with. You can look online for any websites that have values exercises. They all give different lists of words and you can also come up with them on your own.

Step 2. Once you narrow the list down to 20, cut the list down to 10. Work the order so that you have them listed in order of importance to you.

Step 3. Finally, condense the list down to three words in order of importance.

Step 4. Write these words down in a place you can revisit regularly as a barometer for making choices in your life. You can put them on post-its and place them on your bathroom mirror or in your car for regular reminders!

FIND YOUR SONG

Step 1. Once you have your three words, write a sentence that encapsulates how you would like the words to manifest in your life. For example, my sentence would read, "Everything in my life resonates through music and love."

Step 2. You can write two sentences or three if that works better for you. Then revisit the personal mantra section.

Step 3. You can use these phrases as your personal mantra practice if you choose.

Step 4. Write a song melody or a rhythmic rap to go along with your personal sentences and to utilize the full power of your voice.

Step 5. Sing your song for at least five minutes every day until you feel a shift in the energy begin to manifest.

Step 6. Revisit as your life changes and evolves.

Chapter 10 – Follow the Yellow Brick Road

*"No one saves us but ourselves. No one can and no one may. We
ourselves must walk the path."*
-Gautama Buddha, *Sayings of Buddha*

Follow the Yellow Brick Road – yes, it's that simple.

Yellow is the color of the personal power center, the color of the
road and the name of the beloved caterpillar who spun her cocoon
without knowing what was on the other side. Dorothy learned to
trust and follow the path, even though she didn't know for sure
where it would lead. She was trying to find the Wizard to get her
home, so she trusted and surrendered to the journey that
eventually brought her to the ruby slippers and full circle to her
own bed in Kansas. And Yellow eventually emerged as the butterfly.

In Paulo Coehlo's *The Alchemist* (spoiler alert if you haven't read
the book yet), the main character goes on this epic journey of
following voices and signs only to make it to the Egyptian Pyramids
and receive a message that everything he needed was already
inside of him. His journey was all about the lessons and
experiences, rather than the destination.

At various points along the way, he stops and finds love with a
woman who trusts that he will make his way back to her once he's
done what he needs to do. He works for a year at a glass shop where
he cleans and dusts the glass, loses his money, earns more money
and ultimately comes to a place of listening to his own voice – the
one that lived inside of him all along.

The trajectory of the human experience is that, no matter how
epic the journey, you are always led home, either to a physical place

or an internal one. Your journey provides the lessons and allows you to develop the trust that everything you will ever need is inside of you.

These tools are all here to help you learn how to access your inner wisdom.

When I work with individual clients or groups, my intention is to lead people to develop the tools to heal themselves. Ultimately it is up to the person to facilitate his or her own growth and change.

I reflect back to the client what I sense and see in them, because often the person doesn't see themselves the same way that he or she is perceived by others. For example, if I can see that someone is not recognizing his or her own strengths I make it a point to tell them that and reflect back to him or her what I witnessed. I also point out the tools and abilities the client has at their fingertips.

This reflection in itself is healing.

This is also a reminder to seek out this reflection when you feel like you are drained or shut down and need a positive, healthy mirror.

FINDING PEOPLE TO HOLD SPACE FOR YOU

Even though I've been doing healing work for many years, I've always had many people holding space for my own process along the way, reflecting back where I was, how far I'd come and what I needed to do to create the next thing.

I've overcome and transformed many diagnoses step-by-step, including migraine headaches, severe muscle tension, bleeding ulcers, irritable bowel syndrome, depression, anxiety, chronic pain, painful bunion, severe allergies, anemia, frozen shoulder and five gynecological surgeries. Each ailment represented a non-physical wound that needed to be looked at and healed. This also involved voicing my truth with my family and in all relationships. And with each issue a different transformative process took place and a chance to learn and grow emerged.

At every step along the way I went to various healers to help hold space for me. My gratitude for the many healers that helped me get here is immense.

In seeking out your own healing, it is important to use your voice to speak up for your needs and seek out options and modalities of healing that can optimize your healing process. Using your voice may be all that you need, or you might need to find people to advocate for you along the way. My experience has been that the process can be accelerated when you have help.

Whatever path works for you is valid as long as you are listening to your inner voice. You can transform your own ailments and anything that blocks your voice through patience, persistence and cultivating relationships with those who will hold space for your transformation process. The vibrations of chanting, toning and speaking mantras give you the power to heal yourself, and finding the right people to serve as guideposts helps light the way.

The voice has multiple layers and it takes time to let all of the changes sink in. I wouldn't have been able to do the work I do now if I hadn't done the internal practice work myself and had people holding space for my transformation through witnessing the transformation in my voice.

TRANSFORMING IN THE EYES OF THE WITNESS

One of my clients loved to sing, but her focus was dancing. She also worked as a bodywork practitioner and was scared to put herself out there as a singer even though she felt very called to sing.

After just a few sessions, she started using her voice along with the singing bowls in her sessions and received amazing feedback from the participants. I witnessed her, created the healing space and eventually she was able to access parts of her voice that had previously lain dormant.

She overcame her own blocks around sharing her soul simply by doing it and pushing through the fear. She reconnected to that joyful space and continues to use her voice in this way now.

Another client I worked with was more interested in the shaping of his words around how to frame a longtime project to combine digital media with spiritual teachings. Over several sessions of witnessing his process and reflecting back what I heard in his voice, he was able to clarify his vision for the project and how to sell it to investors and participants in a way that made him elated and excited.

He gained renewed vigor for his creation and found his voice in his artistic offering to the world.

I witnessed another client's development over the course of a few years, seeing her for a session once every six months. During that time, she was diagnosed with a mysterious illness where her body and immune system basically attacked itself. As I watched her progress and process, I noticed how she had positively transformed something internally each time I saw her.

The last time I worked with her, she was ready to write her book, had been singing mantras to herself and learned how to clear her house of her own negative energy. She took complete responsibility for anything she was creating in her life that no longer resonated with who she was and took the steps necessary to make the changes.

I bore witness and held space for her to do the work, but she did the work herself.

Her own voice, bravery and courage brought her to the place of knowing when she needed help and reflection and, in turn, knowing when she needed to do her work on her own. She is still healing the disease through mental and emotional development, but she is better able to manage her physical symptoms and her own self-care now.

PATIENCE AND DISCIPLINE WITH SHARING YOUR TRUTH AND SHARING YOUR VOICE

In your own process of connecting more deeply with your voice, the more you share your inner truth, the more you will grow.

Sharing your story, connecting with your singing voice, sharing it with the world and cultivating your creative expression is a journey. Getting there takes time, effort and support.

The path is not linear in the way the Western world may want you to think. The path of the spiritual voice is bumpy and covered in dirt. But if you show-up every day and do your work you will get there. And in the process, be kind to yourself. When you are unable to keep the momentum and need to start over, find the people to help you along the way and hold space for your growth. When you hit a rock, dust yourself off and get back on the path again.

The healing path came to me at a very young age, but I was sidetracked by many diversions along the way. I now see these diversions as lessons, like the character in *The Alchemist*. And I continue to follow my own Yellow Brick Road to the Emerald City that ultimately leads me home, the same road that led me to find my voice, in order to help you find yours.

Breakdowns and breakthroughs brought me here to the most important role of my life: to be of service.

And in service to your process, let's take a moment to recap the 10 steps.

Step 1. Write your Story. Validate your journey by telling your story.

Step 2. Reframe any victim or survivor portions of your story into lessons learned. Choose Your Mantra. Begin implementation of your mantra practice and incorporate this into your daily life.

Step 3. Prepare to Unleash Your Voice by getting clear with your intentions, cultivating courage, looking for the signs that help you allow your path to unfold. Practice the Brain Dump and Diaphragmatic Breathing.

Step 4. Work with the mirror and your internal voices to identify the voices in your head and get clear on your internal dialogue. Then you can begin to change the voices that you don't like or that are not serving you into those that will.

Step 5. Look at your shadow self and shadow emotions deeply. Begin to use them as tools to grow and develop a keen sense of awareness, embracing the full range of your human experience and emotional depth.

Step 6. Learn to work with the chakras to bring your entire body and being into alignment for optimal function.

Step 7. Use the new tools to heal yourself with your voice. Express yourself more deeply through trust, chaos, the primal scream, humming, improvised singing and creating your inner songbook.

Step 8. Integrate all the pieces of yourself into one form. Identify your incongruent puzzle pieces, let those go and build new ones to create a puzzle that matches who you currently are.

Step 9. Transform through seeking help from others. Learn more tools to develop further cultivation of trust, courage and clarity. Learn how to trust the unknown and embrace change. Identify the moments to enter the cocoon and the moments to emerge as the butterfly.

Step 10. Find and seek out places to share your voice, sing and connect with others through music in community.

Before I leave you to journey on your own, I have a few suggestions for how to continue to work with your voice. I encourage you to find ways to share with others, especially in public. If you are drawn to singing more traditionally, find a local community or church choir that resonates with you. This outlet can help you become more comfortable with sharing your voice in a group and connect with people who share your love of singing.

In the spiritual yoga community, you might find local offerings of kirtan evenings, focused on mantra singing in call and response style. Sound baths where people offer toning circles or friends getting together to sing songs and share music are also good outlets for singing in community. You can also buy a singing bowl in your favorite chakra tone (see the chakra toning exercise for the pitch) and begin to sing along with the bowl and play it when you are chanting your mantra.

If you are more inclined to share your voice solo, seek out local open mic nights, plan an evening to perform for your friends and family, or plan a public performance of some kind. You can also go deeper by finding a voice teacher or coach who can help you access the parts of your voice that are stuck. Find the teacher that resonates best with you. Discipline and practice with a guide who will hold space for your process will open more doors with your vocal abilities.

And finally, sing as much as you can, whenever and wherever you can.

From your heart and soul.

Allow your voice to have an outlet, allow your voice to be vulnerable, allow your voice to reflect who you are from the inside out.

Now is the time to get out there and sing:

even if it's uncomfortable,

even if you don't feel ready,

even if the voices in your head are shouting at you not to.

And when you finally find your voice:

you will soar,

you will be heard,

you will move into being the singer that you are.

And YOU are meant to sing!

THE SINGING TOOLBOX

SUGGESTED ACTIVITIES FOR CONTINUING GROWTH WITH YOUR VOICE

Join a choir.

Go to a local sound bath that includes toning for the group and sharing of the experience.

Find a group that sings kirtan.

Take voice lessons.

Plan an event where you can perform for friends and family.

Plan a public performance where you can share song or a story.

Work with a voice coach.

Work with a life coach to guide you.

Reach out with questions or guidance about your next steps if unsure.

Buy a singing bowl and begin to tone and sing with it as a daily practice, connecting with your feelings and expressing them through sound rather than words.

SING as much and as often as possible!

Further Reading

The Alchemist by Paulo Coehlo

Effortless Mastery: Liberating the Master Musician Within by Kenny Werner

The Complete Guide to Sound Healing by David Gibson

Human Tuning Sound Healing with Tuning Forks by John Beaulieu

Tuning the Human Biofield: Healing with Vibrational Sound Therapy by Eileen Day McKusick

The Way of the Peaceful Warrior by Dan Millman

When Things Fall Apart: Heart Advice for Difficult Times by Pema Chödrön

Nonviolent Communication by Marshall B. Rosenberg

Hope for the Flowers by Trina Paulus

The Four Agreements by Don Miguel Ruiz

The Art of Listening 1: A Visionary Guide to Craniosacral Therapy by Hugh Milne

The Success Principles: How to Get From Where You Are to Where You Want to Be by Jack Canfield

Astrology, Psychology and The Four Elements by Stephen Arroyo

Health Building: The Conscious Art of Living Well by Dr. Randolph Stone*Be Here Now* by Ram Dass

Initiation by Elisabeth Haich

The Mirror of Relationship: Love, Sex, and Chastity by J. Krishnamurti

From Rifles to Roses: Memories and Miracles by Iva Nasr

Acknowledgments

Unlock Your Inner Voice was a phrase that literally got locked in my head a few years before this book came into being. I knew it was my path and passion to help people with their voices, but the process of unlocking my own voice needed to come first. Every single time I sang, the key turned a bit more and, through slowly speaking my truth and uncovering the tools to get there, the door finally opened and, with it, this book. So the title emerged as **You Are Meant to Sing!**

There are a few key people that I need to thank who brought me here. First, I would like to thank my mother again, as I did in the dedication. Her bravery in letting me begin to share our story turned into a deep place of healing for both of us. May sharing these intimate details help you also move into a deep place of forgiveness and healing. At the time I wrote the first draft of this book, my mother was still alive and she has since passed on. I am forever grateful that she knew I dedicated the book to her before she passed.

Gratitude beyond words goes out to Elena Zaretsky – my Editor Extraordinaire, dear friend, partner-in-crime and travel companion. She is an amazing writer and editor and this book would never be what it is if it wasn't for her and her hard work and dedication in helping me prepare to unleash these teachings to the outside world. I am so grateful for our ever-deepening friendship and collaborative endeavors.

I would like to thank my cousin and Goddaughter Katy Daixon Wimer whose support as I went through the process of writing this book was remarkable, and for her support in writing my foreword. I also extend gratitude and thanks to my immediate family who lent support along the way, even when disagreeing with me and not always understanding what I was trying to do. To Alex & Megan (Everette), Linc & Brooke (Riley, Jack and Vivien), I am so proud to call you my family.

To my entire extended family – thank you for being part of my unfolding journey and support. I would like to express a special thank you to my 96-year old maternal grandmother Helen Wilson (birthname was "Helane") for all of her listening over the years, and to my Aunts Dawn Donalds and Catherine Wilson for being there in some of the roughest patches. The same goes to my mother's best friend Judy Folstad who I consider part of my extended family.

My deep gratitude extends out to my dear friends Stacy Greene, Adam Morganstern, Sandy Flynn, Grace Oh and Jesse Reynoso who were very much there from the beginning of the book to the final manuscript. I also want to thank my friends Demi Faraday, Jeralyn Talia, Jonathan & Josephine Moerschel (Zoe & Audrey), Leigh & Carla McCloskey, Ben Powell, the choir at First Presbyterian Church in Santa Monica, Daniel Wachs, Amanda Melati Ramirez and Bruce Hartzell who encouraged me as I worked through some of my fears about putting myself out there.

I would also like to thank the participants in my first Unlock Your Inner Voice programs for putting your trust in me and following the process as this book came into being: Scottie Thompson, Inannya Magick, John Carr, Emma Riskin, Haleh Manavi, Laura Alfano Cammarota, Kristi Sandeno, David Lambert, Riesie Stern, Yvonne Hartmann, Audrey Emerson, Emme Paige, Robin Geselowitz and Lana Hermann. Your willingness to go deep and find your voice is inspiring to me.

I would like to thank some of my amazing mentors and fellow teachers and healers who have helped me get to this place through holding space for my process and helping me along the way: Tracy

Griffiths, Gary Strauss, Andre Ripa, Gianna Piccardo Ripa, Anna Dias, Pat Brown, Dawn Yurkovic, Gypsy Gita, Olaf Hartmann, Dana Gioia, Mark Alan Hilt, Ara Guzelimian, Jenny Bilfield, Louahn Lowe, Kate Shela, Paul Hubbert, Kate Hawkins, Jamie Bechtold, David Gibson, Angela Lauria and Iva Nasr, among others.

Finally, I extend my thanks to all of my clients. I feel honored to be able to help all of you on a journey of self-discovery. Watching your growth in finding your voice is my greatest joy.

All my love,

Helane

About the Author

Helane Marie Anderson, author and creator of the *You Are Meant to Sing! 10 Steps to Unlock Your Inner Voice* transformational program and book, began singing as soon as she came out of the womb according to her parents. A songwriter trained as both a classical pianist and singer, Helane has extensive experience in the classical music industry as an administrator. She has held artistic programming positions at both the Los Angeles Philharmonic and St. Paul Chamber Orchestra, served as Director of Composers & Repertoire at renowned classical music publisher Boosey & Hawkes and is currently adjunct faculty at the University of

Southern California (USC).

After spending many years in the music industry, Helane decided it was time to give back and she trained to become a Sound Healer, reconnecting with her original love of singing and healing work. In recent years, Helane has focused on creating workshops that combine her healing journey and the modalities she has studied into a space that facilitates deep healing and letting go through the voice. She has also produced two sound healing recordings, *ELEMENTAL ALCHEMY* and *PAINTED SOUND: A Journey Through the 7 Chakras*, that help to balance the elements and chakras within the body, mind and spirit.

Helane is certified as an Integrative CranioSacral Therapy Practitioner and Massage and Polarity Therapist through the Life Energy Institute/ I.P.S.B, the Institute for Psycho-Structural Balancing in Culver City, CA, with further studies at the Milne Institute in CranioSacral work. Helane holds a certificate in Sound Healing and Therapy from the Globe Institute in San Francisco, CA, has received additional training in sound healing with John Beaulieu and Jamie Bechtold and is a certified vinyasa yoga instructor.

Helane's deepest passion is to share her music and help aspiring singers, speakers and seekers get in touch with their voice and transform!

Website: www.sacralsounds.com

Email: sacralsoundsla@gmail.com

Facebook: www.facebook.com/sacralsounds

Instagram: @sacralsoundsla

Thank You

My deepest thanks to you, dear reader, for taking the plunge to go deeper with your voice and explore your truth within yourself and music. As a special thank you to accompany your continued journey, you are gifted CD downloads of my sound healing albums *Elemental Alchemy* and *Painted Sound: A Journey Through the Chakras at 432hz.*

To receive your download codes, please visit www.sacralsounds.com/youaremeanttosing and fill out the contact form with your information. You will then receive all of the details via e-mail.

May you continue to share your voice and may your journey deepen.

Thank you from the bottom of my heart,
Helane

Made in the USA
Lexington, KY
27 December 2017